Merry Christmas
Lauri —

Love, Mom & Dad 2005

YOU ARE

GOD

GET OVER IT!

YOU ARE
GOD
GET OVER IT!

STORY WATERS

First Limitlessness Edition – December 2005

ISBN 0-9765062-4-6

Library of Congress Control Number: 2005910229

Also available from Limitlessness Publishing by Story Waters:

    'The Messiah Seed Volume I'

    'Love Is Awake'

    'Story Waters speaking in Santa Fe 2005'

To order please visit: http://www.limitlessness.com

For
Shaumbra

Table of Contents

Preface
I Am Free

Freedom is not superior to limitation;
with this realization I am able to choose freedom.

Happiness is not superior to suffering;
with this realization I am able to let go of suffering.

Abundance is not superior to poverty;
with this realization my abundance flows.

Nothing is superior to anything;
with this knowing I step out from
hierarchy, competition, and struggle.

In this state I do not judge life;
therefore I do not feel separate from it.

I am so glad of the diversity in the world;
in its reflection I see my own freedom
to be whatever I wish to be.

We are not here to be one;
we are here to be many.

Through seeing that beyond this illusion we are all one,
we free ourselves to be the many.

I am not tied to any singular path to be a certain way.

I am diverse.

I am ever changing.

I am an explorer of *All as truth*.

Unfolding 1
You Are God

I am God that I am. Because *I am*, I am God. All that has beingness is God. God is being – the choice to be. All that *are*, are God, because to be God is *to be*. God *is*. God is not a thing; it is no thing. Everything is God. God is the all and the nothing. No definition can contain God. God encompasses all definition. Anything that *is*, that possesses the quality of isness, is God. You are the unfolding of the choice to experience existence. You are God.

In saying 'God' I mean *no more* and *no less* than the beingness from which all experience flows. *No more* means I attach no limitation to it – no mechanism of control such as ideology or dogma. *No less* means it is *All That Is*, including all expressions of limitation, such as ideology and dogma. God is the infinite freedom *to be* from which all realities birth. Being that which underlies all that is experienced, God is both the creator and perceiver of all experience. It is that which creates itself – the creator and the created. God is that which you are – the unfolding creation of your own beingness.

The personified God, as represented in many religions, is a denial of our power of creation. Though these religions seek to connect us with an *idea* of God, they also enforce a belief that we are separate from that divinity. They then sell themselves as the one true gateway across this divide, making the route to God pass through their own set of rules. Though organized religion was once a representative expression of the age, it no longer reflects the sense of the divine that people are experiencing. This experience is typified by the feeling of *God within,* and is being reflected in people choosing to form their own personally defined sense of spirituality, rather than taking on the traditional dogma of religion. We are choosing to step back into conscious creatorship.

God is present in all of creation. To feel a sunset is to feel a reflection of God. To fully experience your Godhood is to connect with the power of creation that you are. To fully experience anything is to *be* it. That is what creation is. *Creation is the power to be.* To say God is infinitely free, is to say that God can *be* anything. God is the infinitely free power *to be*. To grasp this is to let go of the idea of God as a person. In you, God *is* a person. In a tree, God *is* a tree. In a river, God *is* a river. What God chooses to be, God *is*. You are that power to *be*. Creation is not external to you; it is your experience of yourself.

You are God choosing to *embody* the power of creation. A person is the choice of God to experience the power of creation as an individual. This is expressed as your individuated free-will. You define your individuality with your free-will. You are God choosing the experience of being you. Free-will is not just the ability to choose between things; it is the ability to choose what you are. Your free-will *is* your power of creation. You are the infinitely free power of creation choosing to be you. This power to create is your Godself – the essence of you. It is that which chooses – that which is choosing you. You are the choice of yourself.

All that you experience flows from your Godself. It is your ever changing expression of being. Your beingness is the experience of your unfolding creation; this includes not only your complete inner experience, but also the experience of your external reality. You are experiencing different aspects of beingness through the creation of your reality. Just as God is the creator of *All That Is* and is *All That Is* so you are both the creator of your beingness and the experience of that beingness. Your experience of the reality you are creating is the expression of your being. Reality is not something separate from you, not something you are contained within. It is the expression of what you are choosing to be. You are not just creating your inner experience of self; you are creating the experience of your complete reality. The word experience is used repeatedly here as what you are, is experience. Experience is being. Experience is. You are not contained within your body, your history, or your knowledge; though they are meaningfully chosen creative expressions, they are not what you are. You are the experience of yourself *and* you are the creator of that experience.

To experience your Godself is to experience yourself as the creator of your reality. To create something is to choose it, therefore to know yourself as the creator of your being is to embrace that you are choosing your experience. To accept you are choosing your experience you must stand in the breadth of perspective that sees the wisdom of that choice. This is to love that choice, which is to love yourself; for if you do not love what you are, how can you believe that you are choosing it? The experience of your Godself is consciously realized through universal, unconditional love for *All That You Are*. Your reality is your choice in this moment and that moment of choice is continually unfolding. The desire of your Godself to be alive is the motion of that unfolding. It is the energy of *I Am*.

Initially it may be easier to see your Godself as the will that guides creation and the creation of that will (your reality) as the experience.

This can be a useful distinction on the journey to the realization of your Godself, because we experience the buffer of time between our desire and its manifestation into reality. However, as you start to experience your unity with *All That Is,* so you will come to see how the desire for an experience, and the experience of that desire, are one and the same. Initially this is felt as the diminishing of the delay between your willing for something and its manifestation into reality. This is to come to live in the *Now,* in the unfolding, where it is realized that there is no separation between your will and its realization into reality. To see through the illusion of time is to see that there is only the *Now.* The *Now* is the unfolding of the eternal moment of creation.

To deny that your reality is your will, is to deny your creatorship – your Godself. As a result of this denial, those areas of your life that you believe are outside of your control are indeed outside of your control, until such time that you take back that power of creatorship. By denying you are the creator you give away your power of creation and, as a result, you will have experiences that you cannot believe you would create for yourself. These experiences are the manifestation of your belief that you are not the creator of your reality. They reflect an aspect of your being that you are in denial of. You cannot cease being the creator, for you cannot stop *being,* instead you simply come to manifest your denial of your creatorship. To *consciously* be God, you must believe you are God.

When you come to realize yourself as the creator, you will see that it was in your creative choice to give away your power of creation that you created all that you cannot believe you would create. All experiences are a choice, even the choice to give away your power of choice; it is your choice to not choose – the freedom of the infinite to be finite. Know however that the choice to take back your power of creation can never leave you. That is the freedom of your will. That is your creatorship. It is your beingness, and it can never leave you, for that is what you are.

You are the choice to be a creator. Nothing except *you* can hold you from the realization that you create your own experience. Ultimately you are the only force in the universe that blocks you, for your will is free to choose anything. To live in limitlessness is to feel the courage to take total responsibility for the state of your life, for it is to know that you are the creator of your life. It is to experience, through the clarity of love for your being, that you are God.

Unfolding 2
You Choose

To know you are God is to realize that all you experience is of your own creation, and that you are free to personally create anything. Just as your free-will is inviolate so is the will of every other being. You cannot create in a way that violates the free-will of another. This is not a limit to your creational power, for in essence you are each and every Godself choosing to have their own free-will. When all are one, then either all are free or none are free. In the complete realization of your own free-will, is the experience of your will for all wills to be free.

In this reality, although we are all one, we experience ourselves as being separate. This reality flows from the original choice we made as God to experience ourselves within the separation of individuality. This separation flows in multiple dimensions; all created by the experience of duality. This is fundamentally experienced as both separation between each other, and as the separation between our inner self and outer reality. At their root they are just one thing – the illusion of separation. This separation, that gives us our individuality, can also be experienced as limitation. We are not however truly limited, as even what we experience as limits are of our own choosing, and how can something be a limitation if it is freely chosen?

We all collectively create gravity as a part of the choice to incarnate in this shared reality. Gravity is not a limit; it is a choice. Even though at times your ego may want to challenge gravity, your Godself knows it as a complete choice upon entry to this shared reality. To accept this is to work within what you have chosen, knowing that it is perfect, because it is what you are currently choosing to be. If you wish to levitate an object the best way to do it is to pick it up. To sit and try and do it with your mind, to prove to yourself that you are God, is to deny your choice to experience a physical reality. You gave yourself a body for a reason – instead of fighting it, love it.

There are so many ways that you can *choose* to convince yourself that you are not the creator of your reality. These are all expressions of the free-will choice to deny your creatorship. Realize that it is a totally valid and reasonable choice to deny your Godhood. This denial creates an amazing flavor of beingness that we have all at some point chosen to experience. To deny your creatorship is as valid as recognizing it.

It cannot be proven to you that you are the creator of your reality, that you are God, because that would be the ability to violate your free-will choice to not see your creatorship. What is offered with this book is a vehicle to embody your choice to consciously connect with your Godself. The realization of this choice is however completely up to you. If you do not want this realization then nothing in the universe can make you realize it. Similarly, if you are ready to experience your Godself, then there is nothing that can keep this realization from you.

That you are reading these words does to an extent imply you are asking for the further unfolding of the realization of your divinity, but equally you could be reading these words in order to experience rejecting them. Whatever your response is, you are the creator of that response. Know that a significant part of the potential of these words to catalyze change is because I, as the writer, am not attached to what your response is. I am not here to convince you that you are God. I know you are God. I know I am you. I know you are safe; you are abundant; you are love. I know you are perfect just as you are, regardless of your response to these words.

I write these words because I want to share my realization of my reality. This is my expression of my creatorship, my Godself, just as your reality is your expression of yours. In my creatorship this is my choice. If the energy of these words triggers a realization of divinity in another I feel blessed, but at the same time I know that for that trigger to occur then that person was choosing it for themselves. With or without me the realization would have happened. Therefore, I do not take credit, I simply feel blessed. I am blessed as out of an infinite number of choices as to how the realization could have occurred, these words were chosen as the catalyst.

I cannot create you. Only you can create you. To realize you are the creator is to realize that you are the creator of your own experience, including your response to this book. You cannot be *convinced* of anything – the very idea of convincing is an illusion created by our resistance to our creatorship. If you need to be convinced then only *you* can convince yourself. The need to be convinced is a barrier of resistance; every word you read will be interpreted through it and will therefore reflect it. You do not need to realize you are God in this life to have succeeded. There is no test. There is just being.

I say with total love that I am not attached to whether or not you realize you are God because I know it does not matter. This realization does not make you any more or less valuable. This non-attachment to outcome is the embodiment of complete respect and allowance for those who read these words. Only through this is there complete freedom of both expression and reception. It is only by writing with complete freedom that I can convey the experience of limitlessness to you, and only through your complete choice that you can hear it.

There can be no proof that takes you from not realizing limitlessness into realizing it. However, once you realize it, then it becomes completely apparent. To understand how this can be, is to realize how amazing free-will is. It is to see that if your power of creation could be proven, then your free-will, and that is to say your creatorship, would be limited. You exist in limitlessness; integral to that freedom, is that freedom is a choice. If you could not choose to experience limitation then your freedom would be a cage. To realize yourself as the total creator of your reality, is something you must decide for yourself. It already is; you are God, but if you want to experience your Godhood consciously then you must *choose* this realization for yourself.

For me this was experienced as the choice to step out of a cage. Now I look back on it, I see how when I was in the cage I hoped that the freedom outside, that sang its song of love to me, would break down my walls and pull me out into freedom. This was the desire for proof – the desire to be saved by something external. This was the giving away of my *power to be*. To stand in your power, the complete realization of your Godself, is to realize that you are you, the cage is you (of your creation), and the love and freedom that calls to you from outside of the cage (your hopes and dreams) is you. This is to realize that you can walk out of any cage you are in, for you are the creator of its limits. It is to realize that if you want to be rescued then it is you that must rescue yourself, for it is only you that is caging yourself. You are the hero and the villain, the jailer and the prisoner, of all your dramas.

To experience the freedom that is inherent to your being you must choose to experience it; and so it is for the love that you are, the joy that you are, and the Godself that you are. You are God. This is my knowing. But whatever your resistance to that idea, if you so choose, it is up to *you* to face it – to 'get over it'. Only you can choose to let in the joy, freedom, and love that the realization contains. To be free is a choice. It is the choice I seek to embody in this book. It is the choice before you.

Unfolding 3
The Illusion

To be born into this reality is to enter a wonderful illusion. This illusion grants us our individualized free-will and our personal reality. To realize you are within an illusion makes this reality no less real and no less special. All realities are simply different forms of illusion. We are one; we are God; but within the illusion we experience the separation of self and other. To our incarnate being the experience of self and other is just how it is – the norm. However, from the perspective of the unity, what we experience here is wholly unique and profound. This kind of physical, temporal reality is a revolution in beingness. To enter it is a gift.

This illusion is one of the most amazing creations in all existence. Within the realization of your Godself is the realization of how uniquely special this kind of reality is. It is to see, without judgment, the beauty of what surrounds you and know that it is of you. To awaken is to be stunned by ideas such as original sin and the notion that we are in some way fallen – cast out of the perfection of Eden. We are not fallen. We are the cutting edge of God. We are pioneers. We are celebrated.

The founding mechanism of the illusion was simply that it allowed the illusion of separation, where the one could be many. At this initial conception point we knew what we were (God) and where we were (in an illusion that granted us our individualized free-will). However, even though we had our individuality, we only experienced it in a comparatively shallow way. Though we experienced self and other, we maintained our full awareness of our unity. In our desire to further explore the experience of separation we chose to enter a collective forgetting of our divinity. Only by forgetting that we were God could we fully identify with our individuality and experience ourselves as separate and distinct. In this forgetting we birthed the ability to be able to look at each other and not know we were looking at ourselves.

The illusion can be imagined as playing all the hands in a card game. If you consciously moved around each chair around a card table, playing each player's hand, then you would know what cards each player has and there would be little enjoyment. If however each chair only carried the memory of its own hand of cards then it would be as if you were playing many different people. Our space-time reality is a wonderful game and each of our bodies is like a chair in the card game. When we incarnate, we generally choose to limit our experience to that of our body; meaning we take on individuality. By experiencing a limited aspect of *All That Is* we are creating new experiences of being. Separation and limitation are not a 'bad' thing; they are the foundation of this reality. They allow the infinite exploration of new expressions of being. They have birthed diversity within unity. You are God playing the most incredible game ever conceived.

When you physically die it is not that your individuality is destroyed. You live many lives. What you are, everything you have been, is carried forward with you. Even though you may not remember other lives, they are present in your beingness, enriching *All That You Are*. Your individuality is yours. It is a badge of honor, and no matter how completely you remember that you are God, that we are unified, you will never lose that badge. You cannot lose what you have been; it is integral to who and what you are.

The original entry into the game, where the knowledge of our Godhood was forgotten, could be seen as the leaving of the Garden of Eden – the leaving of the Unity. The significant difference to the story is that we, as individualized expressions of God, were not cast out. We *chose* to separate. The idea of eating the fruit from the tree of knowledge of good and evil is the representation of entering duality – duality being the splitting of the unity into opposites beyond self and other, such as male-female, strong-weak, beautiful-ugly, intelligent-stupid, past-future, and love-fear.

Duality is the foundation of this great illusion. Within the illusion everything is relative. Up is nothing without the realization of down. Male energy means nothing without female energy to contrast it. To divide something in two you must name both sides. Our perception is founded on these dualistic scales, also known as polarities. These polarities are all symbolic divisions that form both our personal and our collective illusion. They are that by which we choose to separate one thing from another. They are that by which we differentiate our experience and create our beingness.

Since the creation of this reality system we have entered ever deeper into the illusion – further into differentiation, separation, and limitation. The general state of belief that we currently birth into when we enter the game is that we are not God, we are separate, we are mortal, we are purely physical, and that our will is limited. At first glance this may not look so wonderful, but having explored some profound extremes of separation we are now on the journey to returning to remember our Godhood. It is hard from within the illusion to understand just how unique and wonderful this current reality state is. We are God experiencing a state of being that is not only totally new, but from which new states of being are continually birthing.

All realities are in a state of unfolding and this reality is literally an explosion of *the realization of being*. This explosion is reflected in the acceleration we are experiencing in the advancement of our technology. To some it may seem that this new technology is a move away from spirituality, deeper into the illusion of physicality. This is perceiving spirituality from a historic, religious perspective that sees physicality as profane. Spirituality and technology are not separate; they are simply different faces of our beingness. The new technology is the physical manifestation of our unfolding realization of the freedom of our being. It is a spiritual unfolding. Our blossoming communication systems reflect the growing realization of our unity.

As we start to connect back into our divinity we are coming to embody the freedom, harmony, and limitlessness of the unity whilst within the illusion. This is the idea of the creation of heaven on earth. The heaven, the nirvana, which we as explorers of being seek, is not the bliss of the unity. We chose to leave the unity to come here, and we are not just seeking to undo that choice. The joy we seek is the remembering, the awakening, to the realization of our Godself *within* this exciting illusion that we have created.

Many of us are choosing to awaken to our Godself in this lifetime, but this is said with no sense of 'mission'. We are not here on a mission to do anything. There is no way in which it is possible to fail. Life is not a test. We are here *to be* – to be in the unfolding of our beingness. Our awakening is the current natural state of the unfolding of our collective beingness. We are waking up. We are remembering. There is no mission or challenge to do this. It is happening. It is inevitable. We have already chosen it. So just sit back and enjoy experiencing your beingness. Enjoy the ride that is your life.

You are a part of the most glorious wonderful event that has ever been. You are not here by chance. You are here because you have, across many lives, been a part of creating all this. You are not here to observe the wonderment. You are the wonderment; the experience is direct. Allow yourself to experience how wonderful you are. You are amazing.

Unfolding 4
The Unfolding

God is unfolding. You are in a state of unfolding. All realities are constantly unfolding. It is a state of continual birth – an ever evolving state of perfection. There is no hierarchy in this idea of evolution. What *was* is perfect. What *is* is perfect. What *will be* is perfect. You are not becoming superior to what you were. You are remembering more of what you have always been. What you are is freedom, and you are realizing that freedom in ever blossoming ways. You are not becoming 'more' free; you are, have always been, and will always be, infinitely free. You are God realizing the freedom of your chosen state of being – the beauty of your choice to be.

The original creation of differentiation (the illusion of separation) could be seen as a folding. Each fold we created was a part of the journey into division – into individuality. Each fold was a creation of polarity – a way of dividing one thing from another. In this state of folding we moved away from the experience of our unity into the experience of being separate from each other.

Through the illusion, we have explored differentiation. Through differentiation we have explored choice – the freedom of will to choose one thing from another by differentiating between them. Our will has been limitless in this exploration, meaning that *all* choices are possible, even choices such as the choice to see ourselves as wretched and sinful, the choice to hate ourselves and each other, the choice to be lonely, and the choice to suffer. Nothing is denied. There are no limits to the polarities we can traverse such as joy-misery, love-fear, and unity-alienation. We created these polarities and dived into them to experience the uniqueness of being they create.

To some it has seemed that we became lost in duality – that on some level we made a mistake and became trapped in suffering through our self-identification with our minds and bodies. This is a denial of the freedom of our will to be. There is no force in the universe which causes you to incarnate here, other than your free-will choice. You are here because you chose to be. The idea of some karmic wheel that we are bound to is no more than a re-conception of hell – enslavement. To believe in it is a choice, and to believe in it is to live by it. We each live within the experience of our beliefs. Look at how your beliefs serve you to see why you are choosing them.

We pushed against the divine state of unfolding in order to explore profound depths of separation, both from each other and from the unity. This effort against the unfolding illustrates how we did not somehow get lost; it took conscious effort to achieve. It was a choice. The unfolding could be seen as a mechanism that we built into reality, such that if we are not creating division (folding) then there is a natural flow back to the realization of unity (unfolding). The natural flow is not forgetting, it is remembering, but it is not a mistake to forget. The unfolding is not falling asleep, it is awakening, but it is not a mistake to fall asleep. Without effort, you unfold, but it is not a mistake to fold.

To see through duality is to embrace paradox. Just because the natural effortless state is unfolding does not mean that unfolding is superior to folding. You could not be here now experiencing unfolding if you had not entered into the folding of definition. Folding and unfolding are as yin and yang. Sometimes the natural state of unfolding is to fold, and sometimes in folding we unfold. Both are motion, both are life. Whatever you do you are expanding – you are exploring being. You cannot un-evolve. You are like an ever-unfolding fractal. There is no end to what you are.

To be in the motion of the unfolding is to be in the *Now*. It is to have let go of resisting reality and become fully present in the moment. As such it can be seen as a state of allowance. The unfolding is experienced through the allowance of your entire being, including the present manifestation of your reality. To be in the allowance of your reality, instead of resisting or fighting it, is to enter the experience of its unfolding – to enter the flow of life. What is so beautiful is that this flow will always carry you harmoniously towards the realization of your wholeness. The unfolding unifies what has been separated, heals what has been wounded, and frees what has been contained.

To enter the unfolding is to confront the traditional belief that life is a struggle. Within the unfolding life is effortless. You do not have to struggle for what you desire if you let go of your resistance to change and enter the unfolding of your being. This is to realize that ease comes simply by letting go of struggle. As long as you see 'what is' as an obstacle to be pushed against you hold yourself outside of the unfolding.

The very belief that you need to struggle causes struggle. The belief in the need for effort has been ingrained over so many lifetimes that being without it can initially seem inconceivable. On some level we still want toil; we want to know that if we work harder than other people we will get more. We are attached to a level of competition that is shattered by the realization that everything you want can be obtained joyfully and with ease. Effortlessness threatens to undermine many of the ways we use to feel of worth and superior.

Our essential core state is the ease of the unfolding. It is that which *is*, when we allow ourselves to simply *be* – the state of being that arises when we let go of seeking to control reality. It is the feeling that flows from the realization that there is nothing wrong, there is no problem, and nothing needs to be fixed. There is nothing you *need* to do. There is no need, effort, or struggle in the unfolding. This does not mean there is no action; it is that all action in the unfolding is effortless. The unfolding is the state of complete allowance of your being – the allowance of your personal reality to be as it is and unfold as it will.

To enter the unfolding is to let go of judgment of yourself and your reality. To judge an aspect of your being comes from an attachment to your perception of a polarity, such as beautiful is superior to ugly. When you judge a part of yourself as ugly, you are in resistance to your being – in rejection of yourself. Such judgments of yourself, or others, as *needing* to be changed are non-allowance, and hold you outside of the unfolding. When you release judgment and expectation for what reality 'should be' and instead allow 'what is' then you release your being into its natural state of unfolding unity.

All resistance is at its core your resistance to your Godself – the allowance of unfolding to be *All That You Are*. You are the unfolding of your own being; that state of motion; that journey of change. To resist change is to resist the unfolding. It is to resist what you are. It is only through fear (which includes attachment – fear of loss) that you create pain. Allowance is a state of trust in your divinity and inner knowing of your safety. It is freedom from fear. Allowance for your being is love for your being. What births from this is wonderful, is healing, is joy, is that which you seek. If you so choose, it is time to allow; time to allow your being; time to love your being; time to unfold the love that you are.

Unfolding 5
Follow Your Heart

Whatever you do to another you are doing to yourself. They are you, and even though they are expressing a different reality, you are still, in essence, acting upon your own being. In this realization, the concept of karma is simplified from the idea of actions coming back to you over time, to the realization that the effect is direct. All action is of you upon you – all is God. This is to experience the motion of the unfolding. It is to connect with the energy of your Godself at the level of your action – the *Now*. In this state you can clearly see the energy that your actions express and how that energy is feeding the manifestation of your reality.

Your action is integral to your being. What you do, is not separate from what you are. To experience your Godself is to live in the realization of your unity with life. To feel that connection is to know that everything you do has impact. It is to come to know your being through what you choose to do. Your action is not just the end result of a choice; it is the energetic expression of that choice. The energy of your action, which encompasses the choice of non-action, is a potent element of how you create your reality. Your action is not separate from you. Feel yourself in what you do, and you will see what you are doing clearly. If you find yourself dissociating from what you are doing, ask yourself why you are doing it. Choose actions that you want your awareness to be present for.

To unify with your action is to see your action as the expression of your desire. Your *wanting* is the originator of action and determines its energy. Your action is the energetic expression of your desire – one of the most intimate aspects of your being. The energy of your action is not determined by its result. Your action may not even be connected with why you *think* you are acting. The energy of your actions flows from their origin – your heart.

Within the world the result of your actions are the co-created expression of that energy with all the other people involved; so may, or may not, appear in line with your personal intention. Everyone has complete free-will. Other people choose for themselves how they interact with your energy. For example, you may act from jealousy such that you hurt someone, but in co-dependence they may perceive your jealousy as caring about them. Conversely you can act from love to honor someone by ceasing to participate in their self-destructive behavior (which is to cease your own self-destructive behavior) and they may perceive it as cruel. You create in your moment of expression. You do not then control how your creation is perceived.

You cannot fully perceive the energy of what you are doing purely through thought. Mentally we are quite capable of deceiving ourselves as to why we do the things we do. To *think* that you always know why you do what you do, is to be closed to the magic of life. If you wish to know your energy you must open up your most powerful perceptive sense, your heart, and *feel* what you are doing.

The separation of thinking and feeling is something we have qualitatively separated, when in reality they are both aspects of our unified awareness. Because of this separation, the process of awakening often feels like leaving the noise of the mind and dropping into the heart – a move from thinking to feeling. However, ultimately it is about coming to connect with your unified awareness which is fed from *All That You Are*, including the mind. An open heart is the unification of all of your levels of awareness. To act from your heart is to act from your Godself.

To allow your *being* to flow from your heart is to allow yourself to be what you are. It is to know that what you are, fits perfectly in the unfolding of the all. To be what you are is to consciously experience your Godself; this is the experience of your unfolding. To allow this connection is to unify with your Godself. It is to allow your being to unfold from your unified level of awareness. In this you will discover that the message of your heart is to be yourself, and that is to love and honor yourself before all else. You can only love another as much as you love yourself. To love yourself is to love *All That Is*. Love for *all* flows from the love that you experience in your feeling for yourself. This challenges the idea of sacrifice. Many believe that to love means to sacrifice themselves to help others. If your heart guides you to help another then it is your joy and there is no need for sacrifice. Your Godself is in the harmony of the unfolding. In this harmony sacrifice is not necessary. No aspect of your being exists to be sacrificed.

In the loving and honoring of your being, your heart will at times guide you to act in a way that may hurt someone. For example, you may leave a relationship that your heart is no longer in. To leave that person is to love both yourself and them. To stay is to hurt both of you. When your heart guides you to act in a way that hurts another, it is from love, and love is both expressed and received. It is to see that in loving someone you may sometimes, from their point of view, hurt them. Know that just as your Godself led you to the experience, so did their Godself. All shared experiences are co-created; all are chosen. All that flows from your heart aids the unfolding of all. All that flows from your heart is love.

To live in harmony with the world do not let any mental moral code define your actions; let your choices flow from your heart. Realize that no list of rules can successfully be used to determine all actions. In what may appear to be identical situations the heart may in one instance say "yes" and in another say "no". The heart perceives from *All That You Are* and, though your mind cannot always translate what your heart feels into a verbally expressible (mentally justifiable) reason, what your heart conveys through your feelings is based on the most encompassing and unified level of perception that you possess – your Godself.

To perceive through your heart is to perceive through *All That You Are*. It is to perceive with omnipotence. This level of unified awareness can rarely be contained verbally as thought. Omnipotence is not of the mind. It is an arrow that directs you through the feeling in your heart; where it points comes from the knowing of God. Built within you is all the guidance you will ever need. No other being in the universe can guide you as well as your heart. To allow yourself to *feel* your being is to experience your Godself, for as soon as you open your heart that is where your awareness will be.

To learn to feel from the heart and utilize that as your primary guidance is to unfold the freedom, joy, and abundance that you are. This journey will take you through the cages, resistances, and wounds that currently cloak your Godself from you. To heal a wound you must bring your awareness to it. To release resistance it must pass out through your beingness. To open a cage you must first come to see that you are imprisoned. In following your heart it is not that you will never experience pain. However, the pain that you do experience will come from *releasing* pain from your life, rather than from creating new wounds. With each wound released so the entire experience of your being is freer; through this your heart, and therefore your communication with your Godself, becomes ever clearer.

Only a fully open heart can convey the realization that you are God. The mind alone cannot take you there. Logic cannot take you there. Proof cannot take you there. An open heart does not take you there: an open heart is there.

Unfolding 6
Allowance

To be in allowance of your being is to enter the blossoming of your Godself. It is to be in clarity. Through the complete allowance of your being you enter the effortless flow of the unfolding of *All That You Are* – the unfolding of the dream of yourself. The unfolding is the manifestation of your allowance of your heart's dream. It is that which flows from the realization that you are safe to be yourself which includes whatever you are becoming. You are limited by nothing other than your imagination. Unleash your imagination into the creation of your reality.

To be in allowance is to let your being expand without seeking to control its unfolding. Your Godself is the motion of the unfolding and that motion is the love of life. To feel this flow is to feel your beingness beyond the cloak of definition. The unfolding of reality is not separate from you; you are not outside of it. It is you. You are the unfolding. You are the creator of the unfolding and it perfectly reflects your Godself in harmony with all Godselves.

Beyond the excitement of willful, proactive creation is the realization of living within the creative flow of the unfolding *as* the expression of your choice. The unfolding is the will of your heart. To enter the unfolding through allowance is to stand in the unity of co-creation with all life as expressed through your own life. There is no separation between your personal unfolding and the unfolding of the world.

Allowance is neither active nor passive. There is nothing active you need to do to allow, but this does not mean that it is best to do nothing. Allowance encompasses non-attachment to outcome; however it is not about being detached from it either. To be in allowance is to be in the flow of life that runs beneath the separation of duality. To be attached or detached to an outcome is to be within the illusion of separation. Allowance is beyond the polarity of attached-detached. It is simply to allow *being* to be.

Many believe that in order to be of impact they must act with force upon the world. To be without force is not to be without will or choice. To be in allowance is to be without *effort*, but without effort does not mean without action. It is to be in action that is effortless because it is in harmony with the unfolding. For most people entering into allowance takes a huge amount of courage as it involves letting go of the controls (fears) that they have used to feel safe or of worth. To allow your being is to have the courage to be who you are with complete transparency — openness and honesty. Someone in allowance radiates their Godself by allowing *All That They Are* to flow through their being. In this state they are far from passive: they are fearless. To be in complete allowance is to let your being flow without hindrance, and that means without the resistance of fear distorting it. It is the strength realized through being naked and vulnerable.

One of the most fundamental beliefs that separates us from this state of fearlessness is the idea that without effort our world will disintegrate. Essentially this is to have no belief that there is a loving flow to life — an unfolding. It is to see life in purely physical terms, which is to only acknowledge the definition of the illusion. From this standpoint, to step into complete allowance and release control is seen as committing suicide; akin to letting go of the steering wheel of a fast moving vehicle. This view, that without effort things will fall apart, is at the heart of the struggle and competition in this world. It is a war; a war with life; a war with each other; a war within us.

To come to the allowance of your being is to realize that life will support you if you will let go of fearing it. It is only your fear that tells you that this is not so, and while that fear is in operation it will reinforce itself. All consciousness seeks to validate itself, including your fear. Fear tells you that you must *effort* to survive. Fear tells you that you are not safe without protection — that the world is innately hostile. Fear is that which holds the realization of ease and safety from you. But fear is not the enemy; it is that which points you to where you are not allowing. Fear can be used as a signpost to your freedom.

The journey to the complete allowance of your being is a journey through the release of your fears. To enter into complete allowance is a path that is only taken by the most fearless beings alive. It is the path of fearlessness. To be fearless does not mean to never feel fear; it is to face what you fear and take back your freedom that is locked within it. Freedom from fear is to no longer act or choose from your fear. It is to be true to yourself, no matter where you fear that will lead you.

Allowance is to let go of fighting life. This takes far more bravery than making yourself stronger and tougher so that you can fight harder and better. To be without weapons takes far more courage than being in a state of permanent arms. Weapons are generally an expression of fear. Remember however that there is no absolute here. It is not 'wrong' to be armed. It is only when you feel the *need* (emotional need being an expression of fear) to be armed that you are acting from fear. In your choice to not arm yourself do not fall into being judgmental of the choice of another to be armed. To be in allowance is to not only allow your own free expression of choice; it is to equally allow all others their choice of expression. To be in allowance of all beings is to be in the recognition of the equality of all being. Allowance for self is only fully realized in allowance for all.

Through our fears we seek to act upon the world and change 'what is'. Through allowance we open ourselves to be changed by the world through experiencing our unity with it, rather than our fear of it. Within you is both the ability for allowance and fear. Come to see these as manifest in the choices before you. To choose from allowance is to enter the ease of the unfolding through both non-action and effortless action. To choose from fear is to struggle to change yourself and your reality from a fearful denial that you are already beautiful in your unfolding.

To move into allowance, from being in fear, does not take effort, but it is an active choice. You are the only one that can make that choice. To allow your being is to love your being. To allow life to unfold *as it will* is to love life. To love is to respect and honor the right of all being to exist. To be in allowance is to choose from love rather than fear. Fear is the freedom and love that you are denying yourself. To come to choose from love is therefore to give yourself that love and that freedom. Allowance is to love yourself.

To lay down your fear is to face and release it through knowing that it cannot harm you. Your fears are illusions. They are that through which you have separated yourself from the realization of your Godhood. Fear is the cloak through which you have come to feel separate and alienated from the world. To release fear is to let in the realization of your unity with life.

You are not alone. The world does not want to harm you, it wants to love you. It can only do this through your realization of your unity with it, and through your allowance of love for yourself. To love yourself in isolation is a beautiful stepping stone in the unfolding realization of love. Beyond isolated love is the unity of love. You are the world. You are love. Love yourself through the world. Allow yourself to feel the love of the world. Love the world by allowing it. Love yourself by being yourself. Allow the world to love you.

Unfolding 7
Your Story

Your story is that which you know yourself to be — your self-definition. When you describe yourself you are telling your story. It is however far more than a list of descriptive statements. It is an ever changing window through which you both view and interact with the world. Just as your body is a vehicle of your being, so too is your story. It is both the expression and perception of your beingness, reflecting your joys, wounds, hopes, fears, and loves.

When someone tells you their history you discover so much of who they are, not because the events of their life have made them a certain way, but because they are telling you the events with which they currently identify their being. To see your story as 'that with which you are *choosing* to identify yourself' is to begin to see what a fundamental aspect of you it is. It is the expression of how you have individuated yourself from the world around you and from the conscious realization that you are God. Your story not only determines what you present to the world; it determines how you experience the world. A revealing exercise is to list the adjectives you would use to describe yourself to others. For example, if you said, "I am spiritual, kind, fat, intelligent, old, and happy", this not only shows how you see yourself, but it reveals some of the primary polarities through which you perceive the world; namely unspiritual-spiritual, cruel-kind, fat-thin, stupid-intelligent, young-old, and happy-sad. How you describe other primary figures in your life, both liked and disliked, will reveal further polarities.

Your story is not just an idea of yourself that you call upon when necessary; it saturates every aspect of your being, even how you perceive the world around you. When you look out into the world you are looking through the eyes of your story. Your story reflects the polarities which you have identified as being of worth. If you perceive yourself as a victim then you will come to see the world as being filled with victims and victimizers. If you feel the love that you are, then you will perceive the love that surrounds you.

Your story reflects the degree to which you either experience yourself as unified with the world or alienated from it. The greater the worth you assign to the polarities (polarizations) by which you define yourself, the more you will feel separate. This separation is a product of your perception being polarized. Your perception creates the illusion you live within. Separation is the illusion. It is however an illusion that you are freely choosing in order to explore unique states of being. You explore *being* through your perception of it. Your story and your perception are two facets of the creative free-will choice to be what you are.

You are the choice to be the self-identified you. The definition of your story gives form to that choice. Fundamentally you are limitless, but you are currently choosing to experience yourself in a self-limited form – a story. You are choosing to be in a shared reality that is created by many stories. This reality is based upon an illusion, but through our mass consensus the illusion is given great consistency, making it appear totally solid. It is truly amazing to be in a reality that appears to be separate from you in a tangible and permanent way. It is a playground of new experience for God. Never has an illusion seemed so real and created such an experience of individuality.

You express your individuality as a story. Your story gives shape to your experience through not only your self-definition, but through how it shapes your perception. Your perception of yourself and the world are one. How you perceive the world is a reflection of how you perceive yourself. Reality is a mirror of your being. The experience of both reality and yourself come from your perception. Your perception is formed by your story and you are that which is choosing your story. You are the creative free-will choice of your perception and you are living within the experience of that choice. That choice forms not only how you experience yourself, but your entire reality. You are choosing your story and your reality. You are the creator of yourself and your reality. You are the creator. You are God.

You are choosing to be in a self-created illusion, and your experience of that illusion is determined by your perception of it. You are free to perceive it as you choose. There is no separate objective truth to the illusion, beyond your choice to be sharing it with other self-determining expressions of God – other stories. Though a part of being in a shared reality is sharing certain agreed upon parameters, those parameters are not a limit; you are choosing them because you want to experience them. These parameters are the choices that give reality its linear time, an agreed upon appearance of solidity, and its consistency of individuality. They are that which you are wishing to experience; otherwise you would not be here.

By awakening to the realization that you are the creator, the illusion becomes more free flowing and responsive. This is experienced as reality becoming less solid, less consistent, and less governed by linear time. In your awakening you will start to feel less separate, not only from the people around you, but even from the illusion itself. You will see how we are all connected – one inter-flowing story. To awaken is not to escape from reality; it is to enter deeper into the joyful experiences that it affords us.

The realization of creatorship is manifest in the realization of how easy it is to change your reality. To change your reality is to allow the experience of change. As your reality is a reflection of your story, to change your story is to change your reality. To step into your creatorship is to step into change; an ever changing reality and an ever changing story. To realize your Godhood is therefore to let go of having a fixed definition. It is to stop seeking to make your story consistent. You are not your story; your story is your choice in the *Now* of how you wish to experience yourself. Change your reality by changing who you are choosing to be. Release seeing yourself in a singular way and allow yourself to experience *all* ways.

You are in the experience of individuality, but the story you tell yourself of who you are is not your lot for this lifetime. Your story is a choice that you have the power to change. To become identified with the definition of your story is to become contained by it. Realize that if you cease to identify with your story, you will still be you. In this is the discovery of a wider freer you. The you who can be anything it chooses. It is the realization of both the freedom *of* your story and freedom *from* your story. All realizations of freedom are the unfolding realization of your divinity.

Letting go of your story does not mean to lose your individuality. That would mean to return to source. You are not here to return to God; you are God. To free yourself from the limits of your story is to remember that you are God whilst you are within embodiment – within the experience of individuality. In awakening you do not lose that sense of individuality, but it does transform. Instead of experiencing yourself as a singular choice of story, you experience yourself as the writer of your own story, with the power to change it as you will. Rather than being trapped within a story, you live in the realization of whatever story you can imagine. Instead of being one story, you realize that you are potentially all stories.

Your being is infinite. There is no story that you cannot be. You are free to be whatever it is you wish to be. You are an infinitely free unfolding story. Know your story as your freedom and not your cage. You are free. You are an embodiment of God.

Unfolding 8
The Equality of Being

The realization of your Godhood is not about transcending the illusion. It is not about leaving physicality. You did not come to this reality in order to discover it as flawed and then leave. Here is where the most adventurous explorers of being come. The illusion is flawless and amazing. It is perfectly imperfect. It is beautiful. It is ugly. That is what duality is; the ability to see opposites. The idea that beautiful is better than ugly is not an absolute truth; it is a chosen perspective. Nothing in duality is absolute; it is all relative; the meaning we assign to any polarity is freely chosen. To see this is to let go of the idea of absolute truth. The desire for some transcendent, universal truth is a desire to find something reliable and consistent to identify with. In a reality where everything is in a constant state of change, it is the desire to find something that does not change. It is to deny the unfolding.

To embody the realization of your unity with *All That Is,* is to see through the separation of duality, whilst staying within the illusion. To see through the illusion whilst remaining in it is simply a choice. To choose it is to both open a whole new level of experience, as well as close off certain other experiences. Most of the experiences you close off are ones that you are happy to be without, such as fear and jeopardy; however, the vibrancy of fear and jeopardy are a valid choice; just as valid as the freedom that opens up from seeing through duality. One is not better than the other, they are simply different.

To awaken is a state of freedom, but even the idea that freedom is better than limitation is not an absolute truth. To see freedom in this way can be challenging. It is to realize that even something this precious to us is still a polarity. When you see beyond duality you see with the eyes of your Godself, and that is to see the equality of all being. What you choose to believe is not 'the Truth'; it is simply *your* truth. This only diminishes your experience if you have been using the idea of knowing 'the Truth' to either feel of worth to yourself or superior to others. By letting go of the need for the existence of absolutes you release yourself from the cage of perceiving your being in a hierarchical way. You cease to compete with others; no longer finding either them or yourself lacking. This release of judgment is the birthing, into your conscious being, of the freedom of the unified perception of your Godself. To release judgment is to see the equality of being. It is that which reveals the perfection of all life.

As long as you believe that any state of being is 'the Truth', including these words, then you are a slave to that belief. A belief that either end of a polarity is superior to the other is to be caged within that polarity. The competition of duality has become so ingrained in us that we have even turned the unfolding of our divinity into a hierarchy. Many religions are based on the idea that they possess 'the Truth' – a singular path to God. Such a belief system is essentially dualistic, and from within it people are viewed through a judgment of how much they understand this ultimate truth. People at the top then sell themselves as gatekeepers to 'the Truth' and assign themselves status based upon the hierarchy. No matter how much it may be cloaked, any belief that your truth is 'the Truth' is a statement of superiority – a statement of separatism. It is a denial of the equality of the love of God. There is nothing you can say, do, or believe that makes you closer to God than anyone else. You are God.

To see through duality is to see that what anyone chooses is simply their choice of expression. No state of being is superior or inferior. There is nothing that anyone needs to become. There is no ultimate truth governing how you should be. You are an unfolding state of truth that you are freely choosing to explore. To fully understand this is to apply it to itself; seeing through duality is not superior to not seeing through duality. To consciously embody your Godself, such that you are no longer contained in the hierarchy of duality, does not make you superior to those still choosing to explore duality.

To embrace the realization of the equality of all being is to step into the freedom and limitlessness of your being. Without this realization, though your will is still in essence free, much of it becomes predetermined by your beliefs. If you believe that there is an ultimate truth that we are here to reveal, then you naturally become tied to discovering that truth. The journey from not knowing 'the Truth' to knowing 'the Truth' becomes a hierarchical scale. Your choices, instead of being made from your heart, are made from the idea of moving up this hierarchy. To realize the equality of being is to be free from a type of separatist thinking which defines certain choices as being superior to others. In the realization of the equality of being, all choices of 'how to be' are equally valid, and as such, are freely available to you because you are not trapped within a judgment of them. This is to choose from the awareness of your Godself. It is to choose from limitlessness, rather than limitation. All of the truths that we hold so dear are simply beliefs that we are choosing with our free-will in the creation of our experience.

The choice to experience superiority, which is a denial of equality, is the choice to live within that perception. This creates a personal reality which reflects the polarity of superior-inferior. To choose superiority is to equally invite inferiority into your life. With all duality being relative you cannot have one end of a polarity without the other. To judge one end of a polarity to be superior is to be contained within that judgment. That judgment, whether positive or negative, is a statement of self-identification. The judgment creates the experience of duality through a belief that the ends of a polarity are separate. The strength of your belief in that separation, conveyed in the absoluteness to which you believe one end is superior to the other, determines how tangibly that polarity is manifest in your reality. Your dualistic beliefs are the creators, not the result, of the duality that you experience. You are not trapped within duality. You are the creator of duality.

This sense of being contained in a polarity comes from being identified with it through your beliefs about it. When you see the equality of all points on the spectrum of a polarity, you encompass it with your perception, as opposed to being contained within it. By not identifying your being with a polarity, you are not restricted in your perception of it. For example, if you have a strong belief that people are of greater value if they are intelligent, your perception is then limited by your judgment of the polarity of intelligent-stupid. Everyone you meet is perceived through this judgment and you experience a sense of separation between yourself and those that you perceive to be of significantly different intelligence than yourself. This experience of separation is from within your own being; its boundary is an aspect of the definition of your story. You are that which chooses whether your beliefs separate you from the world around you, or unify you with it. There is no right or wrong to this; it is simply to live within your own beliefs.

When you release a polarity it is not that you will never experience it again. You will perceive the polarity only when you choose to focus on it, rather than having it inextricably overlaid on your perception like a tint. In the freedom of seeing beyond duality comes the ability to see the beauty in all states of being. This is a form of clarity that is not possible when your perception is colored with judgment. With the realization of the equality of all being, the co-existence of unity and diversity within your being ceases to be paradoxical. The freedom to be both unified (both within yourself and with the world) and yet separate (expressing your own unique and diverse individuality) is birthed. Diversity is not contrary to unity.

Unfolding 9
Unfolding Your Story

Within the illusion we cloak our limitlessness in a self-limited identity – our story. Our infinite source, that contains all possibility, is expressed outwardly through each of us into definition. You are an expression of this possibility and are free to express yourself as you choose. Whereas some choose a tightly defined expression, others choose a broader, more fluid expression. Neither way is better than the other. Each carries its own unique flavor of being.

To express yourself in a tightly defined story is a form of focusing your being. Examples of this type of life would be someone married to their work, the devoted housewife who lives for her family at the expense of her dreams, or someone who lives within a rigid military structure. This can be seen as a specialization of being, where the idea of a role is strictly adhered to, producing its own unique experience. To see such life roles clearly is to see them without judgment of their limits. All stories carry their own unique exploration and gifts whether they are characterized by restriction or freedom. We have all lived many lives, many within highly confined stories, and when we did it was a perfect choice. The journey of a life spent traveling can be as expansive as the journey of a life spent in prison.

Your story can be seen as a circle of beingness extending around you. Inside of the circle are the types of experience that fit within your story – your idea of who and what you are. Experiences that do not fit your story lie outside the boundary of the circle. The more identified with your story you are, the more rigidly you live within its limits, with the boundary of your story being both clearly defined and enforced. Having tightly defined limits brings a sense of reliability through predictability. By not challenging us, the experience within the circle comes to feel safe – a comfort zone. For a person resistant to change, experiences that are inside the circle are allowed, and those that are outside are resisted.

Currently the pervasive state of being in this reality is one of not feeling safe. This has led to people trying to create a sense of safety by establishing a strong identity with firm boundaries. We naturally feel safer when we feel we know exactly what we are and what we are not. We assert our self-identity not just to the world but also to ourselves. Our stories have their own consciousness (this could loosely be seen as the ego, or more literally, as a self-preservation instinct) and that consciousness acts to preserve and protect itself. It is the consciousness equivalent of the physical survival instinct, which is the consciousness of our bodies to protect themselves. This self-reinforcement of our identity is greatly increased when we identify purely with our story, rather than with our Godself. To become so self-identified with your story, that you see it as your absolute truth, is to turn its definition (the boundary of the circle) into a cage. This is said with the understanding that for many, the limits of a cage can be experienced as comforting.

Our self-preservation instinct was a wonderful tool to guide us whilst we were unconscious of our Godself. It acted as an automated mechanism, giving a sense of solidity to our blossoming sense of self. It allowed our self-identity to maintain a sense of consistency within the flow of the unfolding. This self-preservation instinct is neither for, nor against, the flow of the unfolding; sometimes being in alignment with it and sometimes not. It only resists the unfolding when the natural flow threatens to change our story in a way that triggers our fears. Though this does create resistance, it is not a negative thing. This instinct is an embodiment of our desire to be alive in a reality of individuality – our desire to experience a sense of self. It has been integral to our exploration of separation. However, if you are now choosing to consciously connect with your Godself, it is appropriate to change your relationship with this instinct, such that you can enter into your unfolding with ease rather than resistance.

To free this instinct is not to destroy the ego or the mind; it is to see your identity (the circle) as an *expression* of your Godself, rather than as being what you are. This is to let go of identifying yourself with your story and to instead begin to identify your incarnate self with your Godself – beyond the created, you are the creator. The effect of the unfolding is therefore seen to be both the expansion and fading of the circle that delimits your story. Instead of the circle of self-definition being a fortress that you are inside defending, it becomes your choice of expression in the moment – a choice that you are not bound to. In this state of allowance, when the flow of the unfolding brings new experience into your being, then that experience is welcomed rather than resisted. To be in allowance is to be open to the experience of change.

To be open to change means to be open to change in both your inner self and your outer reality. All change, whether it is inner or outer, is a change in your story. To be in allowance of the unfolding is to be open to your story changing. To the self, the unfolding is the unfolding of your story. Allowance is therefore to allow your story to be experienced as a *state of change,* rather than a set, defined singular state. As long as you identify your story as being who you fundamentally are, then the amount of change that you can consciously assimilate is minimal. When you are identified with your Godself, knowing your story to be but an expression, then you can assimilate change with ease. Your allowance of change is a reflection of your freedom to be.

When you are in a rigid identification with your story then you are in resistance to your unfolding. This is because the energy you put into your story feeds the self-preservation instinct that seeks to limit change so that you can feel secure and stable in what you are. To release your self-identification with your story is to take back your energy from that survival instinct and free your being to be whatever it chooses. It is to allow your experience to be more fluid and more creative.

The boundary of the circle of your story can also be seen as the illusion of separation – the veil, the very fabric of duality. The fainter you allow the boundary of your story to become, the more you will see through the illusion of duality back to the unity. The line does not entirely disappear because you are choosing to embody your Godself, rather than return to the unity. It does however become more permeable and transparent, such that you can simultaneously experience your unity and individuality. The line also becomes entirely free flowing such that whatever you wish to experience can easily be embraced by your being, and that which you have fully experienced can go on its way.

Your story is the vessel that shapes the feeling of your experience. You are a sculptor, sculpting the experience of you. Instead of being the whole block of marble, you are the ever changing sculpture revealed from within its potential. The limitation of your story is not felt as a restriction when you realize the freedom from which you are creating yourself, and the freedom with which you can change. This is the beauty of beingness. To not see your beauty is a denial of this freedom. Realize the freedom of your choice to be, by realizing how beautiful and perfect your current choice is. You are beautiful.

Unfolding 10
Love Fear

We easily allow experience that is in alignment with our story because we feel safe in territory that we know. Through the safety of our knowing we feel in control. However, by already knowing the territory, our experience of it brings little change, because it is a quality of experience that we have already assimilated into our being – into what we know ourselves to be. We easily allow familiar experience as it does not threaten to change us. The effect of only living in the known is to come to live in a story that is our container, rather than an expression of the effortless exploration of our freedom of being.

Outside of the known, outside of your story, is the unknown – experience that you have not yet allowed into your beingness. What holds these experiences outside of your story is your resistance to them. The fabric of resistance creates the boundary wall of your story. To be in the unfolding is to freely allow the beingness of whatever is unfolding. To allow the unknown is to allow your Godself to unfold into your conscious awareness.

Your story is the known. Outside of your story is the unknown. The membrane of your resistance separates these. To let down your resistance is to take down the barrier between you and the unknown. It is to enter the threshold of revelation where the unknown becomes known. It is a threshold where inspiration, expansion, and change birth into being. It is revelatory consciousness. It is through this state that the most profound ideas and art have birthed into the world. The greatest accomplishments of humanity have all come from creators freely allowing the unfolding of their beingness. In more routine circumstances, this state of revelation helps to clarify everyday decisions, and inspires you to see ways in which you can unfold your being. It is a state of simplicity, where choices are easily made with clarity from the heart.

This kind of revelatory consciousness sounds like a place we would all like to be, and yet it is a state that people rarely attain. Initially to go into this state is to stand *within* the wall you have created between your story and the unknown change that you fear. It is to stand within your resistance to that change. It is the proverbial 'jumping off the cliff' feeling, not knowing where you are going to land – not knowing who you will become. All resistance is, at its root, fear of change – fear of the unknown. Even the primal fear of death is the fear of not knowing what the experience of death will be, not knowing what lies beyond. To come to truly know anything is to come to not fear it. Nothing that is known is feared.

The scope of each of our stories is different. Some people have a wide range of experiences that they can engage in, where they remain secure in what they are; others have a narrow range. What both have in common is that the boundaries of the story are defined by resistance. Resistance is the moment when the freedom of your being recoils from an experience out of a fear of what it contains. This is the experience of touching on a limit in your story. In this moment you have the choice to maintain your story and go with your resistance, or you can open your heart and go through the resistance to let the experience in. In doing this, an aspect of the unknown becomes known, what was once resisted becomes allowed, and the freedom of your being unfolds.

Generally we believe that if we are resisting something then it is a useful self-protection. This idea is one of the greatest locks on the cage of a singular story. To believe that all your fears are useful self-protections is to agree with the existence of the bars of your cage. To see this is to realize that you are not only the prisoner of any cage you experience, you are also the jailer. The bars of any and all cages are bars of fear, and you are the determinant of your fear. To say that you choose your fear is simply to restate that you are the creator. You are God, and in the acknowledgement of your creatorship such walls are not needed, as it is to trust in yourself not to choose what you do not wish to experience. You are the architect of your story, and you create the walls that cage you out of your resistance. A wall is simply something that resists you walking through it. In creating your story you build walls where you fear whatever is beyond that point. A wall is not wrong; it is simply a statement of fear. Fear is not wrong; it is that which allows our separation. Beyond your fear is your unity with life.

To face your fear, and stand in your resistance, is therefore to take down a wall you have created. It is to redefine the territory of your being and allow it to become an ever changing, ever expanding landscape. It is to realize that the walls with which you have defined yourself are not what you are; it is to cease identifying with them. Though we tend to let our fear define us, by letting it govern our behavior, it is not what we are. You are not your fear. Your fear is a tool you have used to express your chosen definition. You are that which chooses. You can choose to determine your fears to be valid or you can choose to release them.

Fear is not a bad thing. This is such a profound and yet subtle point; within its understanding lays a great freedom. Fear is not an external force out in the universe that is trying to hurt you. To be experiencing fear is not a mistake, and it does not need to lead to suffering. Fear is an energetic state that you use in the creation of your beingness. Whereas love is attraction, fear is an attempt to create repulsion – separation. Fear is that which allows a barrier to be created in the free flowing freedom of being that is our Godhood. It is a tool of definition.

Within duality fear is the opposite of love, and as such, it is as significant to the formation of the experience of this reality as love. This is referring to dualistic love which can be focused, as opposed to universal, unconditional love which is an honoring and acceptance of all life equally. You cannot have attraction without the existence of repulsion. Just as fear has been a force with which you have limited your being, so you have used love as a force to free your being.

To see fear in this light is to see it as a purposeful tool and not a ball and chain. You have not done anything wrong in limiting your being through fear. You have done it from a desire to have the unique experience that living within a story gives you. All the walls in your being have served you well and are to be honored. To take down a wall from this understanding is to do it with ease, because you are standing in the recognition of yourself as the creator of that wall. You cannot take down a wall that you see as being a mistake.

To come to face your fears from this empowered standpoint is to do it without suffering, because you are in recognition of your Godhood. You are not overcoming any devil or force of evil. You are not overcoming anything. You are simply choosing to stop defining yourself with fear. You are not forcibly knocking down walls. You are ceasing to create them, by choosing to no longer live within the limits they represent. To realize you are the creator of your restrictions is to realize that you are free. To release your fear is to come to live in an ever changing landscape that is defined by the love of your heart, rather than the fear of your mind. Love your fear and it will unfold into your freedom.

Unfolding 11
You Are Safe

To feel fear is to not feel safe. It is to feel that you are in danger. To feel in danger is to believe there is something outside of you that is capable of hurting you. It is to believe that your being is in jeopardy. The experience of jeopardy arises from the belief that you are finite. The illusion that something is finite is an aspect of the illusion of duality where the infinite can be seen as fragmented and limited. Fear and danger are therefore products of the illusion. The idea that you are not safe is an illusion. You are God. You are immortal. That which you are cannot be destroyed. Though you may choose to pass through physical death, it is not the end of what you are. Death is a choice that your Godself makes to leave embodiment. Death is but the end of the illusion that you are finite.

When you believe that your story is everything that you are, then change is a threat to what you perceive yourself to be. Fear feels so tangible because your self-identification with your story is in jeopardy. So in terms of what you *believe* yourself to be, you are in danger; your beliefs are felt to be in danger of changing. To say that your life is in danger is to say that the illusion that you are separate is in jeopardy, because if you die you will discover that you are not separate from anything. The only thing that can ever be destroyed is the illusion. The destruction of illusion only ever results in clarity. This does not mean that all illusions should be destroyed, simply that the destruction of them can never harm what you essentially are. Experience does destroy/transform/change your beliefs, but you are more than your beliefs; they are only the window you are choosing to look through.

If you believe that your body is who and what you are, then it is quite logical to fear it dying. We fear losing anything that we are attached to. Attachment is fear – the fear of loss. To be attached to something is to have identified your being with it. It is to identify it as a part of your story. Attachment is to take an aspect of being and come to believe that without it you are not complete – that you will not be whole. This leads to the fear of how you will be changed if you lose it. Out of this fear of loss you build walls around what you are attached to, in an attempt to hold it close.

Attachment is not love. Mutual love holds things together through a co-created attraction. Attachment is fear based, not love based. However it is not that you should be detached. In relation to the fear of the death of your body, it is not that you should become detached from your body. Detachment is as polarized as attachment, just in the opposite direction. Your body is a beautiful part of the expression of

All That You Are in this world. Along with every aspect of you, your body is to be loved. Love your body, but do not attach your identity to it, such that you fear its loss or change. Love your body as the ever changing reflection that it is. Allow your body to be as it is.

People live in fear because they do not believe that they are safe. Attachment is an expression of that fear (an attempt to create a feeling of safety), and as such, is one of the main building blocks of a self-limiting story. Just as we build walls with our fear to keep certain experiences out, so we build walls of attachment (fear of loss) to hold onto things that we have self-identified with. To seek to possess an outward state of being in this way is to deny that you can choose to be any state of being within yourself. To know you are God is to know that you are everything; you are infinite. Only through the belief in a finite supply does the need to possess arise. Only in the belief that resources are limited do we come to compete for them.

The fear that flows from jeopardy is not from an external source; it is a reflection of your attachment to your story, a part of which is your body. If you are afraid of your body dying then that energy is a part of your being, and as such, will in some way be reflected back to you, usually through a perceived physical threat. This is to live within a story that is defined by fear. It is to live within the experience of your fears. That which you fear internally is experienced as something to be feared in your external reality.

To know you are God is to know that all fears arise from the fear of realizing that you are infinite. Our self-preservation instinct fears limitlessness out of the belief that it will destroy our sense of individuality. You are you; that cannot be lost. Nothing can be lost for you are everything. You are a singular individual and you are *All That Is*; you are the realization into being of this paradox. The only fears that are existent in your life are fears that arise from the unknown change that you will go through on your journey to realizing that you are an embodiment of infinite freedom. Your attachments are your denials of your Godhood – your wholeness, your safety, your unity with all things, and your limitlessness.

The ways in which you deny that you are God, that you are love, are expressed as fear. To experience your unity with all life is to know that all that is outside of you is you. To know you are everything is to know that there is nothing to fear. You are completely safe as you are the source of your fears. Your choice of story is the root and expression of your fear. Do not fear yourself.

There is no external force that is seeking to harm you. There is no danger 'out there'. There is no 'out there'. It is all you and you are love. You are God. You are safe. To realize that you are God is to realize that all your fears have only ever been projections of your denial of your Godhood, arising from the belief that you are separate, alone, and finite. All fear is a part of the illusion of duality. You have only ever hurt yourself through believing that you can be hurt. This was not a mistake. It was a wonderful experience – an exciting roller coaster ride. But now, as you come to see through the illusion, so you see through to the safety that you are. The foundation of allowance flows from knowing you are safe. It is to know you are the creator and to trust that you will not hurt yourself.

Safety is not an external condition; it is internal. When we are in fear we build walls around us, fearing what is 'out there'; believing there is something that will hurt us if it gets the chance. We imprison ourselves out of the belief that our prison will keep us safe, when all it does is cage us in with our fear. Nothing in life has caged you but your own fear. All that limits you is of your own creation. You create limits to protect you from what you fear. What you fear is being limitless.

If you feel fear rather than safety, then that fear will be reflected in your unfolding experience. The more you let the unknown into the known the more you will transform your fear into safety. Let go of the idea that facing your fears needs to be a painful experience. Though we do not generally like the experience of fear, we identify with it because we believe that it protects us. Through a belief in danger, fear is seen to keep us safe. We believe that to be without fear will lead us to hurt. This is how fear maintains itself. Fear is no more than the fear of the unknown.

As you connect back into the realization of your divinity, and come to identify your beingness with your Godself rather than your story, fear will fade from your reality. You will come to live in a world where you feel safe to be who you are. Foster this feeling of safety within your being; it is your Godself. To allow yourself to feel safe is to allow yourself to feel that you are God. God is safe.

Unfolding 12
The Fluidity of Synchronicity

The journey from seeing the world in purely physical, objective terms, to seeing it as a changing reflection of many individuated wills, is one of allowing a sense of fluidity. Just as attachment to a static story creates rigidity in your inner being, that rigidity is also mirrored in your experience of the outer world. Reality reflects both your allowance of it and your resistance to it. To allow fluidity in your being is to experience fluidity in reality.

To allow the unfolding of your being is to allow the fluidity of experience. One of the first signs of this fluidity will be through the appearance of synchronicities in your life. A synchronicity is a meaningful coincidence, and reflects your openness to the magic of life. For instance, you happen to meet someone who spontaneously tells you something you were looking to know. Such a synchronicity on its own could just seem like a surprising coincidence. However, as you step into the unfolding, synchronicities will come into your life with ever increasing frequency, often reinforcing each other. For example, you may be deciding whether you should take a trip when you bump into a friend who tells you that they just got back from a wonderful vacation in France. Next a truck drives by with a picture of the Eiffel tower on its side. Then you open a newspaper to find a special offer on flights to Paris.

Synchronicity is your Godself speaking to you through the medium of your reality. With any synchronicity there is always the choice to either see it as random chance, or as a potent confirmation that there is far more to reality than the physical. When you are within the unfolding, synchronicities can build up to levels that can shake apart a traditional solid view of reality. To be open to synchronicity becoming a significant part of your life is to let go of seeing the world in purely physical terms. There is no external force that either denies or grants you synchronicities. If you do not experience them it is simply the honoring of your choice to view the world in purely tangible, rather than magical, terms.

Your perception is not objective; typically it acts to support, and therefore reinforce, your idea of the world. To believe that the world is purely a physical system is to live within the experience of that rigid belief, and the fluidity of synchronicity is rarely experienced. If you do not believe in synchronicity being anything but random chance then you will only experience synchronicity at a rate that you can comfortably explain away as random chance. Your story is always honored; this is why the decision to change your story can only come from within.

Synchronicities are your Godself communicating with you. They strongly point to the underlying interconnectedness of life. They are therefore threatening to a purely physical point of view. The easiest way to bring synchronicities into your life is to come to trust in your intuition and gut instinct. This *choice to validate* your inner feelings leads you to experience synchronicity. This is expressed most beautifully when two people, who have the means to help each other, meet in the manifestation of a win-win situation. To open your story up to embrace synchronicity is to awaken to how magical reality can be. Synchronicities are neither withheld from you, nor forced upon you. They are potentially around you in every moment. To experience them you must simply *allow* their potential to be.

A high occurrence of synchronicity and a purely objective view of reality are incompatible. Reality is a subjective experience that you are creating, not an inescapable objective experience that you are trapped within. Science is moving towards this realization through the exploration of quantum physics; but until the full ramifications of this viewpoint are embraced, there will be a whole level of reality that science will not perceive. The belief system from which science creates its measuring tools (its perception) is currently too rigid to support the realization of a non-objective universe. As with any story, science will continue to confirm itself until it is ready to loosen its thinking and let go of its need for a separate, objective truth. How scientists measure the world will always confirm the validity of that type of measurement. Just as with science, your story will always confirm itself. How you perceive creates what you believe to be true. You see what you are looking for.

To open yourself up to synchronicity is to let a profound level of communication into your life. Synchronicity can aid you in very practical ways, such as in answering a question when you are in doubt of yourself. The means by which the response to your question appears may be subtle or incredibly obvious. The more you open yourself to the extraordinary level that synchronicities can manifest, the clearer they will become. There is no limit to how your Godself can communicate with you. All perceived limits are of your own creation. The profundity of asking for a clear sign and distinctly receiving it just moments later is not to be underestimated; such an occurrence can seriously shake up your view of reality. It is to ask

God a question and receive a response. Allow the flow of synchronicities into your life at a pace you are comfortable with. To acknowledge synchronicity is to birth great change and clarity.

To understand synchronicities is to realize that you are creating them. Synchronicities convey the unified perception of your Godself. If you are asking for clarity through synchronicity then you cannot be attached to the answer you will receive. The degree to which you are attached will cloud your perception of any answer that you receive. Synchronicity is not a tool to feed your story. If you are looking for confirmation and it does not come, then you are not being given confirmation. Usually you will get a sign that affirms this, but often we block seeing what we do not want to be true. To be in a synchronistic flow is to be receptive to listening to your Godself, no matter what you are being told. To be receptive is to be open to anything. To listen without fear is to perceive with clarity.

Once you have opened yourself to seeing beyond the solid veneer of the physical world, through to the underlying freedom of potential that can rise up through synchronicity, then reality becomes more fluid. Allow time for this process, not because there is a limit, but because the experience is more enjoyable if you give yourself time to assimilate the change it will bring. The degree to which you allow yourself to experience the fluidity of reality is the degree to which you are allowing yourself to experience the innate freedom of your being. Allow the fluidity of life to unfold at its own pace. There is no race. Enjoy the journey.

A rigid reality gives rise to many unique experiences. It allows you to feel safe in what you know. We feel safe with solidity as it is consistent – less open to change. To allow in fluidity is not to destroy all solidity. Fluidity-solidity is but a quality of being that we can express in different ways and in different areas of our life. A part of freedom is the freedom to choose solidity. Let your experiences of rigidity be something that you consciously choose with your free-will, rather than being the cage of a belief that the world is purely physical.

You are experiencing your choice of perception. Reality is as solid or as fluid as you believe it to be. Reality is as solid or fluid as you want it to be. Choose.

Unfolding 13
Sovereignty

To realize that there are no limits to your being is to release the limiting beliefs with which you define your being. Many of our limiting beliefs have been carried over many lifetimes, and have become invisible assumptions as to how reality is. In unquestioningly accepting their limitations we limit ourselves. We become slaves to these beliefs as they invisibly affect the choices we make. We ignore their caging effect, believing that it is simply the way life is. To cease to question is to cease to explore. It is a sign of losing touch with the knowing that you are the creator of your reality. We only cease to question limitations when we believe that we are powerless to be free of them. To know that you are the creator of your experience is to know that you are not a slave to any element of your reality. You are the sovereign creator of your being.

The limitlessness you are moving towards embodying is the realization of the complete freedom of your being. It is to move from being within a world that contains and restricts you, to being in a world that you are harmoniously co-creating. To be in limitlessness is to know that there is no conflict between the mass reality and your personal reality, because we are all one. All conflict in the world is a choice made by the participants to experience that conflict. To believe that conflict with the world is necessary in the creation of your personal reality is to experience that conflict as the reflection of your belief. Your beliefs are all manifested in the world before you. They can either free you or enslave you.

If you do not believe that you can create, then that belief is the very limit that stops you creating. You can only create what you believe you can create. If you cannot believe that you can be rich without struggle, then you will struggle to be rich. There is nothing external inflicting this struggle upon you. If you desire riches, and struggle is the only vessel you will let yourself believe that wealth can arrive in, then you limit yourself to only receiving wealth through hardship. You live within the experience of your beliefs because you create within the context of their limits.

Your story is not just what you present to the world; it is not just how you perceive the world; it defines the limits of your creational ability. Your story is the embodiment of your beliefs. It is the foundation from which you create. The limits of your story not only define the limits of your inner being, they define the limits of the reality you experience. This is how intimate your internal self and your external reality are. You are your reality. The boundary of self that you experience between the inner and the outer is an illusion. You are one with all that you experience. You are God looking at itself.

Even though your story is the vessel through which you limit yourself, there are no innate limits to what your story can be. Your story is the means by which you have taken the limitlessness of your Godself and limited it into something separate and defined. Creation is an expression of the freedom of your being, even when you are creating limitation. To allow yourself to create in new ways is to allow your story to change into something new. To free your story is to free your ability to create. Redefine your reality by changing the definition through which you experience yourself. Rename your story.

Creation is naming. Naming is the giving of definition. This reality is the creation of definition; it is where God experiences itself within definition. In this world you are surrounded by huge amounts of named energy – that which has already been created. You are free to work with this energy and manipulate it into new forms. Our belief that this reality is finite has led to this being the primary way in which we create, because we see all energy as already being in existence. This is the basis for conflict. When we believe that energy is finite then we feel we must compete for it. This belief in the need for competition creates a reality of competition. The wars through which we have sought to enslave each other have been our exploration of the reality created by the belief that our resources are limited.

Usually we try to change something by rejecting it, but in rejecting it we are denying that it is a part of us; we thereby cut ourselves off from our ability to release it. To reject something is to interact with it as a limit, from a disempowered perception of it. To accept that you created something does not mean that you cannot desire to change it. Accept your reality to empower yourself to change it. To accept your reality is to cease to interact with it as a barrier. Your reality does not act to limit you. Your reality is you. If your reality appears to be limiting you, then you are limiting yourself through your perception of it. Your perception of it flows through your beliefs about it.

You are only a slave to that which you enslave yourself. You do this through holding self-disempowering beliefs. No force can enslave you except yourself. We have all explored slavery, each of us playing both sides of the polarity. Let go of the guilt of enslaving, and the pain of being enslaved. Allow yourself, without shame, to see that you have experienced both states. The basis for this choice was the unfolding of our understanding of freedom. We discovered that to enslave another is to be enslaved ourselves, and that to limit another is to limit yourself. We unfolded our freedom through limiting our being.

As long as you identify your being with either enslaving or being enslaved, you are perpetuating the energy of slavery. We have been there; we have done that. Help release it from the world by releasing your identification with it. Do not fear that you will repeat it. Know yourself to know that you no longer need to choose it. This is not a polarity you need to explore any longer. You do not need any person's power except your own. Accept your own power to realize you do not need anyone else's. This is the realization of sovereignty. You are the master of no ones being except your own. The need to enslave arises from the denial of sovereignty. Only those that feel powerless internally seek to control others externally. To embrace your sovereignty is to have released the master-slave polarity.

One of the greatest realizations of our freedom is that you do not need to compete for energy. Reality is not only what is before you; that idea is to reduce *All That Is* to a physical box. You are surrounded by an infinite supply of yet-to-be-named neutral energy. The potential of this energy is only limited by your belief as to what you can do. This energy field is a reflection of our infinite source. Only the belief that you are a slave to the circumstances of your reality holds you from releasing the potential of this energy field. To tap into it is to realize your sovereignty because is to know that you have all that you could ever need in the limitless dominion of your own self-creation. To reject reality is to be a slave to it. To accept reality is to stand in the sovereignty of your creatorship, and thereby be connected to your power to create your experience without needing to control or possess any other. You are the infinite potential of the energy field; there is nothing else you require in order to create.

To know the freedom of choice you have over your beliefs is to come to realize that there is no aspect of reality that you are bound to. There are no shackles to which you do not hold the key. There is nothing that you need to serve. There is nothing that you cannot let go of. There is no limit to the potential from which you can create something new. You are free. You are sovereign.

Unfolding 14
Resistance is a Brake

Resistance is a brake against the unfolding and it is only ever your foot that is on that brake. This brake may be experienced in many ways, such as fear, a practical obstacle, or the shackles of attachment. Resistance has only one source – the being that is experiencing it. You can disguise its origin in an infinite number of forms, but only you create your resistance. No matter how intricately you weave the manifestation of your hindrance, to create a tangled web where many forces seem to have conspired to halt you, the route out of resistance is simply to take your foot off of the brake. You are the only force that ever stops you. This is not to say that there are no other forces in the universe; it is to say that they cannot affect you without you giving them that power.

In order to take your foot off the brake you must first come to acknowledge that it is indeed *your* foot that is on the brake. To deny that you are the braking force is to deny that you are the creator of the resistance you are experiencing. It is to deny your power to lift your foot from the brake. You cannot wield in your beingness that which you do not acknowledge you are.

The degree to which you acknowledge yourself as the creator of your reality is the level of creatorship you have over your reality. That which you acknowledge you have created you can change; this is through the experience of your unity with that creation. To believe that external forces are imposing their will on you is to give away your power of creation to those external forces. If you do not believe you are a creator then you will live within a reality that reflects this. To not be the creator is to be that which is created upon. It is to be a slave. Reality is a mirror of your beliefs. It is through your beliefs that you create your reality. To realize this is to realize the freedom and fluidity of reality. Change your reality by changing your beliefs about both it and yourself.

Along with the allowance of synchronicities, the acknowledgment that it is only ever your foot on the brake of your life is one of the easiest ways to experience the fluidity of reality. Rather than working to actively create something new, get out of your own way and allow the unfolding to occur. As such you are not struggling to make something happen; you are simply allowing what is already happening. Going with the flow of the unfolding is effortless. To cease to push against life is to feel your unity with it. Experience reality responding to you by letting go of your resistance, and thereby experience its intimate connection with your inner state of being; the connection that gives reality its fluidity.

To take your foot off the brake is not to forcibly smash through the barriers before you. To see them as solid in this way is to reinforce that solidity. Instead, realize that your barriers are being created by your resistance to what is unfolding. See that the energy of your resistance is coming from your desire to control the change that is unfolding. Resistance is an attempt to control. This control comes from the fear of pain that you believe you will experience if a certain outcome manifests. You therefore seek to control reality to bring about whatever outcome you judge to be positive. This does not however mean that what you perceive as the negative outcome was about to occur.

When you seek to control reality you block the unfolding, even if your desired outcome was about to happen. Attachment to an event having a particular outcome is fear of the whole event unfolding. We just as readily hold from us what we do want by fearing what we do not want. Control, being a form of separation, always has two sides; to push in the direction you do want is to equally enforce what you do not want; this is how harmony is always maintained. There is only that which divides equally and that which unifies equally. All imbalances are an illusion.

To release the brake is to realize that you are in fear and that through your fear you have sought to control the divine unfolding of your being. Control arises from being attached to an idea of what you believe 'should be' happening. This is a denial of 'what is' happening. When 'what is' happening starts to conflict with what you want to be happening you have a choice; you can either accept it as the unfolding, or you can see it as a problem that needs to be corrected. To see it as the unfolding is to know that, even though you may not yet understand why, it is perfect and meaningful that it is happening. The reason will become apparent when you are ready to accept it. To see it as a problem that *needs* to be corrected is to deny the perfection of your creatorship and enter a struggle against your own unfolding.

To see the perfection of your life does not mean that you will never experience discomfort. Releasing a cage can be painful, but if you desire freedom then it is perfect to release it. To see the perfection in something painful is to view it with the eyes of your Godself. It is to see the whole picture. Discomfort arises when you deny your creatorship; this discomfort is perfect, as it highlights your denial. This does not mean that you should accept discomfort and thereby never act to change anything. Discomfort points you to a change that you are not allowing into your life. By allowing that change into your life, the experience of discomfort will be released. Within the unfolding there are many actions that can flow from the heart; this action never seeks to deny 'what is'. Action that flows from the heart honors the current state of whatever it is transforming; it is action that flows from affirmation, rather than rejection – love, rather than fear.

Let go of seeking to take action to stop what is happening. It is far simpler, and therefore more effective, to allow the unfolding. The unfolding will always carry you towards the realization of your freedom. Let go of control and trust in yourself. To trust the unfolding is to trust your Godself. Your Godself is within your unfolding. Trust your Godself to guide you through the unfolding of reality, even if what is happening on the surface is not what you would consciously choose. Surrender. Surrender the conscious desire to control. Surrender your fear, and fall into the love of the universe.

Take your foot off of the brake of your life and surrender the unfolding of your reality to your Godself out of the knowing that you are your Godself, and that you love yourself. Realize that you will never give yourself more than you can handle, and what you do give to yourself will always be perfect. Know that the love that you are, the love of your Godself, is all around you; it is you. Love your life, rather than fearing it, and that love will permeate your reality. Let go of the *need* to have your foot on the brake. The brake is your fear; it is the desire to limit yourself out of a fear of what you are. You do not need to fear what you are. You do not need to fear where being *All That You Are* will take you.

This is the time of awakening. There is no secret process you need to discover to awaken. There is no mystery. Simply let go of your fears and be yourself. This happens naturally when you allow your life to unfold. It is what happens when you stop resisting life. You are awakening right now. It is inevitable. It will take as long as it takes for you to realize that you are safe, that life is wonderful, and that no brake is required.

Unfolding 15
Let Your Creation Be

You are the unfolding of creation. Within every seed is the energy and motion of its own unfolding. A seed does not need to work to become a flower; it simply allows itself to be, and it becomes a flower. Though you have the ability to engage in the wonders of active creation, you are like the seed in that you already contain a complete and wonderful journey of unfolding. There is nothing that you need to create or change to experience this. When you birthed into this reality you created everything you will ever need. The sun and water that a seed uses are provided to it freely, impartially, and without restriction. Similarly, you are surrounded by a limitless potential of energy that is available to you through your unfolding. You are the creator of your own unfolding. You are free to continue creating to your heart's content, but there is nothing more you *need* to create.

One aspect of entering the illusion of separation from our Godself is that we lost touch with our feeling of completeness – the realization that we already possess everything we will ever need. We lost our sense of being whole; instead coming to see both the world and ourselves as separate, finite, and limited. The illusion of lack birthed from this idea of finiteness, and we entered the belief that we needed to toil in order to survive. The story of being cast out from the Garden of Eden represents our forgetting that we are surrounded by all the sustenance we will ever need. This was the entering of the illusion of lack. Though we became blind to our abundance, we have never left the nurturance of the universe. Abundance surrounds us; open your heart to see it.

From the illusion of finiteness came the belief in finality. We entered the illusion that we could die; from this birthed the drive to live – the survival instinct. The loss of the unity between our self and our reality became solidified by seeing reality as separate and indifferent, instead of being a fluid nurturing reflection of our own love. Our fear of death became reflected in external reality becoming an obstacle. In making reality an opponent we entered the relentless cycle of struggling to survive.

The struggle for survival is now reflected in the belief that we must constantly work in order to stay afloat. We fear that unless we are in continual effort, others will move ahead of us, and what we have built will fall apart. It is as if we see ourselves as continually treading water; believing that if we stop kicking our legs we will drown. This is to be blind to the natural uplifting motion of the unfolding. To feel the unfolding is to know that if you stop kicking, you will effortlessly float. To feel your Godself is to feel the undercurrent of support and love (as opposed to chaos and deterioration) which underpins your life. To feel the motion of the unfolding is to feel the love of God — the love of your Godself for your incarnate being.

Our effort, the very thing that we believe keeps us afloat, is in fact the very thing that pulls us down. Through the power of our belief in the need to struggle we have become blind to the innate ease of life. The belief that we must kick our legs to stay afloat creates the feeling of being pulled down that we are kicking against. This is an example of how beliefs become a cage, because if you stop kicking you will, if it is your belief, initially sink. Therefore, even though the innate nature of reality is for you to float, a belief in the reality of sinking will override this. The belief that your natural state is to sink is a form of resistance to the idea that life can be effortless.

All fears are forms of resistance to the realization of your Godhood. We *worked* hard to create our individuality. We created powerful beliefs to maintain our sense of self in the face of the unfolding. This was not a mistake. The belief that you will sink without effort was an amazing tool of creation. Through it we formed a unique type of reality; we realized and explored amazing levels of individuality. It is only now, if you desire to return to the experience of your unity, that it is felt as being a cage; but even this is not a 'bad' thing, because you can now have the amazing experience of breaking out of the cage of that belief. To have believed all your life that you needed to struggle, and to now discover that life can be easy, is an exhilarating experience. Enjoy it. Enjoy it to realize it.

The idea that you do not need to struggle in order to create is a fundamental shift of consciousness. It is to change a cornerstone of your story. To switch from effortful creation to effortless creation is to re-evaluate your very way of being. So now, if you feel ready, if your heart resonates, here is an exercise to face your fear, challenge your resistance, and thereby disperse your belief that life is difficult. It is simply to let go of effort, to cease actively creating, and that is to stop seeking to change your reality.

This exercise is not something that is going to take effort. It is going to take the release of effort, and that in itself is to be effortless. This is an exercise in letting go, letting go of control. To release struggle is to face the fear that your belief in the need for struggle has been founded on. It is to open yourself to change one of your foundational beliefs – one of your deepest beliefs about what reality is, and about what and where you are.

Realize that, as with all life, this will be an unfolding process. You will gradually come to see areas where you can make the choice to stop struggling against reality, and instead accept it as it is. Realize that in accepting something, this does not prevent it changing through its own unfolding. You do not need to *will* things to change in order for them to change; all things are naturally in a state of change. As you allow your being to unfold you will go deeper into the subtle ways in which you have been pushing against life through seeking to change it. By choosing to allow life, instead of disputing it, the fears from which you were previously acting to change reality will be revealed.

Through allowance you will come to see the distinction between effort and courage, because to cease to struggle is to confront the fear that you will sink. To allow yourself to go under the water is to allow yourself to face unknown change; it is to face the unknown inside of your being. This is the allowance of the emergence of your Godself into your conscious awareness. Have the courage to be you. Allow the love that will support you; allow that which will make you float. Let go of struggle and its feeling of sinking. It has served its purpose. The courage to go under the water is the motion to float. Face your belief that you will sink, in order to experience floating.

The message here is that living, which is creation, can be effortless. One of the best ways to shift from the energy of the struggle for survival to the realization of ease, is to stop creating. In doing this you will be allowing yourself to experience the love and support of the unfolding, which is the realization that the universe wishes to lift you up, rather than pull you down. It is in this nurturing energy that survival fears can be let go of and then, when you feel ready, you can return to proactively creating if you wish. One amazing thing you will discover is that the experience of your seed blossoming in the love of the unfolding is so effortless that you will not be in any rush to return to proactive creation.

You will have to stretch your imagination to imagine a reality that is more succulent than the events of your innate unfolding. Joy is not something you have to work for. If you so choose, joy is what you are.

Unfolding 16
Let the Shit Hit the Fan

To believe in the necessity for struggle is to resist effortlessness. After living with struggle for so long it can be hard to believe that it is not necessary. To allow effortlessness into your life you must face and release the beliefs in struggle that separate you from it. These beliefs are the walls that have kept you from the realization of ease. The freedom, love, and support of your Godself are always reaching out to you through the motion of the unfolding. To enter this ease is to allow change. It is to change your story and that is to let change into your story – the change that you have been resisting.

As you allow the unfolding into your life nothing but wonderful things will happen; however, initially this is quite unlikely to be your perspective. All the walls with which you have defined your story are the creation of resistance to an aspect of your being (an aspect of life). They represent your effort. To lift your foot from the brake is to take down these walls. This is why it is wonderful: you are literally birthing freedom into your reality. The initial face of this freedom will however most likely be felt as the experience of the shit hitting the fan!

The motion of the unfolding is a motion of change. For as long as you have believed in effort, you have been resisting the unfolding of change. The effort of resistance is most commonly expressed as trying to keep something the same when it is in a natural state of transformation. Within a motion of change, to stay the same takes effort. To change through the unfolding is effortless. To push against the unfolding is to struggle. This can be seen as being in a boat on a river. If you wish to stay in the same place then you must paddle upstream against the current – if you wish to not change you must expend effort. To float downstream is to stop paddling – to change takes the release of effort. The feeling of struggle is perfect because its feeling of discomfort is the perfect message to convey to let it go. Feeling tired is a way in which you body tells you to rest. Discomfort is not a punishment; it feels uncomfortable to help encourage you to release the resistance that it represents.

The walls with which you have defined and contained yourself apply a rigid framework against the fluidity of your being. When you come to release effort from your life these walls will begin to disintegrate; not through your effort, but through the release of the effort that you were expending to create them. As these walls come down, the change that has been trying to unfold will start to come into your life; that which you have been resisting will come to be.

It takes an endless expenditure of effort to sustain an unchanging story. To try and block the unfolding is to try and dam a river that never ceases to flow; eventually change always emerges. Resistance through attachment, where we cling to keep reality a certain way, creates the greatest walls. The pressure that can build up behind these walls can be incredibly strong; this is in proportion to the strength of the resistance. These barricaded areas can be seen to be our shit – meaning our deepest issues, our most painful wounds, our shame, our guilt, and our fears.

Everyone has shit; everyone shits; shit happens. It is that which we seek to deny about ourselves – what we are ashamed of. Our shit is the areas of our being that we most avoid, believing that the pain there is permanent – intrinsic to us. Our shit is pain that we have internalized – self-identified with. Shame and guilt arise when we internalize a painful event by regretting it. To lament or regret an event is to reject it. Shit is internalized self-rejection which is experienced as self-loathing. It is to believe that a pain that we are carrying is unalterable. It is to be resigned to live in pain. We carry our pain locked away in the closets of our being, and we often end up expending more energy through our avoidance of acknowledging it than on any other area of our being. Maintaining our shit takes a lot of work. To awaken is to release this effort and face your shit.

When you embark upon the journey of releasing effort you will naturally begin with the less intense areas of resistance, such that you can gradually release the change of the unfolding into your life. As you start to feel safe, the strength of the resistances that you are ready to release will increase. Eventually, if you remain in a state of fearless allowance, your deepest shit will surface. That which you have been trying to prevent happening in your life may well happen, or it will not happen. Either way you will free yourself from the fear of it happening. Those things that you have been working so hard to avoid will emerge into your reality for resolution; to allow this change will be to allow the experience of the shit hitting the fan.

One example of this would be people leaving your life. These would be people who you have been trying to keep in your life when your relationship with them has run its course and it is time to move on. Huge amounts of effort can go into denying that a relationship is over, or in trying to prevent another person leaving; this is a form of control that arises from the fear of losing them. One of the qualities of change is both the birth and death of relationships in your life. You cannot only birth relationships. As with all things, that which has run its course must be let go of, in order to birth what is new, fresh, and exciting. The fear of not knowing what lies beyond the passing of a relationship keeps you locked in patterns that are no longer serving you. To realize your unity is to realize that nothing really dies. From the level of your Godself there is no finality. Though a relationship may end we can dance that dance again as many times as we wish. Enjoy the dance, but allow the faces to change. Do not attach your identity to other people. You do not need to be attached to them to share in their beauty. Share through love, rather than attachment.

Attachment to a relationship can occur at many levels. It can be present in trying to keep a business alive that is ready to be let go of. It can be in keeping someone alive in their sickness when they are ready to pass on. It is common for terminally ill people to stay alive for their friends and relatives when really they want to let go. In doing this they allow the needs and dependencies of others to dictate their life, instead of following their heart. You are never helping anyone when you do not follow your heart. It is to feed the attachment, and therefore dependence, of another person through your own co-dependence. Co-dependence is to seek to stay in a static co-created pattern out of a fear of what will happen if that pattern is released.

To let the shit hit the fan is to face your fear. To some extent the experience will be the manifestation of your fear. Do not however fall into believing that this means it needs to be painful. You will have the choice to be able to perceive it as pain. There will be a sense of loss, but fundamentally it will be a loss of the walls that have contained you. If you can allow yourself to experience it in this light then the experience will be one of liberation.

Liberation is the experience of your Godself birthing into your conscious incarnate being. Within it you will find what you have been looking for. You will discover that all the effort that you put into your walls was in fact holding from you everything that you have ever wanted. Beyond what you have been trying to prevent happening you will discover what you have wanted to happen. That which you seek is contained within that which you fear.

In your shit you will find your treasure.

Unfolding 17
The Individuation of Being

The experience of struggle is the manifestation of resistance. The external manifestation of your internal resistance creates the experience of reality being resistant to your will. The limits of your beliefs about the freedom of your being become manifested as restrictive limits in your outer reality. The walls with which you have limited and defined your story are experienced externally as obstacles, complications, practical difficulties, and even physical barriers.

Struggle and resistance are one. Struggle cannot exist without resistance. Without something to push against you cannot struggle. It is the belief in the world as an opponent. Just as your story limits your internal being, it also creates the boundaries of your external reality. This experience of reality being resistant to your will is the manifestation of the belief that reality is in some way separate from you, instead of being an intimate reflection of what you are. The degree to which you resist the idea that your reality is the experience of yourself is the degree to which you experience reality resisting you, rather than supporting you. That very resistance is a wall that you have built between your perception of reality and the experience of yourself. It is an energetic wedge that separates you from the experience of your unity with the world – with *All That Is*.

If reality instantly responded to everything you desired it would be easy to see it as a reflection of your being; it would be like watching your reflection move in a mirror. Resistance creates the experience of discontinuity between your inner experience and your outer experience (the reflection) that leads to reality feeling like an obstacle. This discontinuity creates the illusion that reality is separate from you; as such it is an aspect of the experience of individuality. It allows us to both define our story internally, as well as individuate our feeling of self from the world. It is not that one set of resistance forms your inner boundaries and another set of resistance defines your outer limits; you have one pattern of resistance and it forms all boundaries. Your inner walls are mirrored in your experience of external reality. In this light, resistance can be seen as a powerful tool through which we created the experience of individuality.

The world is the mass expression of all beings that incarnate (individuate) here. It is a consensual reality which acts as a shared medium through which we interact with each other – the meeting point where individual realities intersect. The world is not solid and objective; it is a co-created intersection of all participants. As we change our personal realities the world changes in its reflection of us.

From the level of realizing that we are all one it can be said that we create the entire world. From the level of your incarnate self it is only your personal reality that you entirely create. However, through your personal reality you can interact with and change the world. You shape your personal reality through both creating anew and through choosing which of the diverse expressions in the world you wish to experience. You then shape that experience through your choice of how you perceive it. Your choice of perception is in itself infinite in scope. There is no such thing as an objective perception. Everything is different depending on how you choose to look at it. No two people's perceptions are ever the same. Even though you are a part of the mass reality, your personal reality remains your own creation.

The world can be seen as the mass expression of all beings within it. We are each God – each the world. You have access to all the creation that flows from the world. The world is unfolding just as you are. Your personal unfolding feeds the unfolding of the world. Often people attached to the *idea* of 'being spiritual' see the physical world as ungodly; this is an expression of separation. They look away from the world to look inside for God, and indeed God is within, but it equally lies out in the world. Internal and external are one; their perceived separation is a part of the illusion. You cannot unify with love within, if you deny the love outside of you. In the experience of unity, nothing is separate.

The world itself is a level of individuation between you and the source unity. To choose to individuate as a human being you pass through the choice to be on this planet; you pass through the choice of individuation that is this world. This is to agree to share certain parameters, such as physicality and our form of time. You then form your individuality through your unique pattern of resistance to the world and allowance of it – the choice of your story. Through your choice of resistance and allowance you choose which aspects of the world you identify with and which you externalize as being separate from you.

Internally your resistance is experienced as the walls that define your story – your individuality. Your resistance is your belief in your limits. More precisely, it is the choice of which aspects of *all* being you will allow into the experience of your *personal* being. To see resistance clearly is to see that it is not negative. It is simply a mechanism through which your choice of being is expressed. There is, quite literally, a world of experience out there, and through your walls of resistance you determine how it flows through your being. Through your free-will you chart the course of your life, through which experiences you allow to flow into your being, and which you resist. Externally your resistance is the barrier that you hold between yourself and the world in order to experience your identity as separate from it. Your belief that you are separate even forms the physical parameters of your being.

Many people have had the spontaneous experience of being unified with their environment. Though it may only last for a moment, it is a startling insight into the many levels of perception that straddle the scale from feeling completely separate from the world to feeling completely unified with it. What shifts your perception on this scale is nothing more than your allowance of the realization that you are one with all life. The more you resist this unity, the thicker the barrier you create, and the more separate you experience yourself as being. There is no wrong or right to this. It is simply a choice of viewing angles, each giving a unique experience in the exploration of being. Sometimes it is exciting to stand back, and at other times it is most enjoyable to be directly involved.

The universe is the physical manifestation of *All That Is*. Our planet is the manifestation of all the individuated expressions of will (beings) that have ever, and will ever, exist here. You are choosing to experience a limited portion of that experience as yourself in this lifetime. That limited portion of experience is not what you are; it is the choice of how you wish to experience yourself in the *Now*. This is to say that you experience yourself as your story, but you are not your story; you are that which chooses your story with infinite freedom. Your beingness is both your internal experience of yourself and your experience of the external world. These are one, but through your resistance to the realization of unity (which is simply the choice to experience individuation), you experience a separation between your inner self and your external reality.

In returning to the realization of your Godhood you are coming back towards the experience of unity. This is experienced as the breaking down of the separation between yourself and the world. It is to cease experiencing reality as being resistant to you and instead experience it as being the vessel of your unfolding. The world is where your chosen life is happening. Enjoy the world.

Unfolding 18
Transforming Resistance Into Clarity

Having your internal resistance manifest in your external reality is simply to live in an experience of your chosen definition. We are here learning about beingness by being. Reality is our greatest teacher; not because it somehow concocts clever lessons for us, but because it shows us our beingness. All lessons are only ever a mirror. Reality does nothing but reflect to us what we are choosing to be.

There is no external force that sets up lessons for you with an expectation that you will learn what you are doing wrong. You are not living in a reward and punishment system. There is no right and wrong; what we feel as right and wrong is but our realization of, or separation from, the love that we are. You are living within the choice of yourself. If through your choice of beliefs you choose a definition that is painful, then you will experience pain; that is the only reason you ever experience pain. It is not wrong to experience pain. It does not mean that you have made a mistake. To accept what is being said here is to let go of the idea that there is a force other than yourself shaping your reality. This is to take complete responsibility for what you are and stand fully in your own power of creation.

There are many forces in the world; every person is a creative force, and though other people may inspire or catalyze you, you are the ultimate creator of your personal reality. Others can only affect your reality if you choose to let them. We came here to not only experience ourselves but to experience being with each other – to catalyze and diversify (but not create) each other's unfolding. The choice of who you allow into your life greatly shapes your reality. To awaken is to realize that you are the determinant of which energies you wish to interact with. If the experience of another person is hurting you, then reality is reflecting that you have given away an aspect of your self-determination to them. Choose with love for yourself who you share your life with. All beings are to be respected, all beings are teachers, but to have them in your life is a choice. There is *nothing* that necessitates any specific person being in your life.

Coming to see that external reality is a reflection of you is not necessary for the unfolding of your being. We originally came here to forget that we are God and experience living in a world of external forces, conditions, and limits. We wished to explore our beingness in the guise of an external reality. To unfold your being through the use of effort, force, and struggle is not only a completely valid way to explore existence, it also births realizations that are unique to this way of being. This is the beauty of reality; it allows us to explore our own beingness under the illusion that we are exploring something separate and distinct from us. The world grants us infinite perspectives.

To move into the recognition of reality being an illusion is not to transcend or graduate. It is to choose to awaken to the illusion and thereby come to interact with it in a new way. To awaken to the illusion is to become more conscious of what you are, but 'more conscious' is not superior to 'less conscious'. It is amazing to awaken, as it transforms your perception, but your level of awareness is simply a choice; it is not a prize that makes you superior. Superior is a dualistic separation; to awaken is to release this belief in hierarchy.

Once you become aware of yourself as an energetic being, living within the reflection of your choice to be, then you can redefine your relationship with struggle; understanding that if you wish to resolve an issue with external effort that option will always remain a valid choice. For many however, the release of struggle and effort is a welcome change as it is experienced as freedom. To transform the struggle in your life is simply to come to see those struggles with clarity. You cannot release struggle by either rejecting or resisting it, because that in itself is struggle. This is why the understanding that it is not inferior to struggle is important. As long as you are judging something you are struggling against to be negative, then you are resisting it. This barrier of resistance stops you seeing what you are resisting clearly. This is because the only thing you are ever resisting is yourself and resistance is a denial of that. The very idea of struggle is one of experiencing a separation between yourself and what you are struggling against. It is a medium of separation. The more you struggle the more you are denying that what you are struggling against is you. To release struggle is to see that your struggle is an aspect of your being that you are resistant to experiencing. The more you resist something the less clearly you see it. This lack of clarity, this clouding, is what allows the resistance to exist.

Resistance is manifest in the belief in the need for effort. The resistance in yourself and the resistance that you feel in reality are one. By coming to see the beliefs you have in the necessity of struggle, you will discover your internal resistance. Sometimes we can blind ourselves to something internally, but when we look externally it becomes obvious. This is to come to experience reality as a teacher instead of an obstacle. When you allow in the idea that all struggle is simply the manifestation of your own resistance, then your struggle becomes your clarity, because it tells you about your being.

The obstacles that you meet in reality are the manifestation of walls within your own being. To come across an external obstacle is then to gain insight into a boundary within your story. Develop your inner sense of resistance so that you can recognize when you are struggle in your life. The more sensitive you become to being resistant, the quicker you can stop feeding that resistance with your energy. To become aware of your resistance is to disperse it, and allow in the change that it was blocking. The very effort that you put into pushing against an obstacle is the exact energy that creates the obstacle. As this becomes clearer it is seen that the actual obstacle which you are struggling against *is* the effort that you are expending. You are only ever pushing against yourself. Reality is the reflection of the energy you are putting out. When you resist, reality resists you. When you push, reality pushes against you. When you allow your being, reality allows your unfolding; this is felt as being supported in your choices.

To see your reality clearly is to see it without the distortion of resistance. To allow your reality is to see your reflection in it clearly. Allow your reality by accepting that it is you that creates it. If you cease to resist reality you will come to see that you are choosing it with love, for it is with love that you are exploring being. The experience of suffering flows from the rejection of your reality, which is the rejection of your choice to be. To reject reality is to stand outside of your power of choice, the essence of what you are. That which hurts, enslaves, or limits you externally, is a reflection of how you are doing this to yourself through your beliefs about, and feeling for, your own being.

To see an obstacle as a symbol of your resistance is to release that resistance. What was an obstacle becomes a teacher. It is to see that all obstacles are reflections of your being; by seeing them as such you are better coming to see yourself. When you realize that the only force that is pushing against you is you, then you are empowered to release the limitation it represents. You can only let go of what you acknowledge you are creating. To reject something is to resist it. To acknowledge your unity with something is to allow it. That which you allow unfolds. To acknowledge that you are the creator of your own barriers, is to experience them dispersing in the motion of their own unfolding; their unfolding is your unfolding. Your reality is the energy of the love that you are cloaked inside of your resistance.

Unfolding 19
Releasing Violence

To experience abuse, whether it is psychological, emotional, physical, or sexual, is to experience the energy of violation within your being. All violation is a form of violence. The energy of violation reflects the strongest denial of our Godhood. Indeed it is acts of violence that most lead people to believe that either there is no God, or that we as human beings have completely fallen from what God is. Violence is a powerful, intense, and intimate experience and is at the root of many of our wounds. A wound is an area of our being where we experienced pain that we felt to be too intense to handle; we therefore surrounded it with a wall of resistance to cut ourselves off from feeling it. However, in sealing off the pain, we then carry that pain in a wound that must eventually be reopened and healed.

From an energetic perspective, to violate another is the same as being violated; it is to experience the illusion of free-will being violated. Regardless of whether you are the victim or the abuser, it is the manifestation of the belief that your will is not completely free – the denial that your free-will is inviolate. Your Godself cannot be violated. However, you can experience violation within the illusion, as your incarnate self can, through its story, experience itself as separate from your Godself. Even though it is only within the illusion, the experience of violence is totally real. To call it an illusion is to say that your Godself (the you that remains unified outside the illusion of separation) is not harmed. However, through identifying with your story, instead of your Godself, you are identifying with the illusion and the pain of the violence is fully experienced.

Whether you are inflicting violence or are its target, at its root is the belief that your free-will can be violated. If through your story you desire to violate the free-will of another, you will attract to you another person that equally believes their free-will is open to violation. Together you will experience the illusion of you violating their free-will in a mutually co-created event. Outside of the illusion of separation it is seen that both participants are choosing the event. This is not to say that they both want to experience pain. The choice occurs at the level where the belief in violation was chosen; the violent experience is the reflection of this belief. The experience of violence shows all involved that they are, in some way, holding a belief in the validity, and therefore the reality, of violence.

The experience of violence is one of the most intensely painful experiences in this reality. This is because the belief that you can be violated is a statement of extreme separation from your inviolate

Godself. The intensity of the pain of violence is a lynchpin for many people in their denial of their creatorship. The experience of being violated is the most common point where we deny responsibility for the creation of our reality. This is because violence is such a painful experience we cannot believe that we could be creating it. To understand how you could be the creator of your own pain is to see how, when you are deep within the illusion of separation, your choice of creation flows from beliefs that *you have chosen* in the past, rather than your conscious awareness in the present. This is to not be living in the *Now*. It is to choose from your beliefs rather than your conscious awareness. It is to choose from the absolute and static, rather than from the fluid expression of freedom that you are – that which is within your heart. To awaken is to become conscious of the effects of your beliefs. You are then able to see, and thereby release, beliefs that are creating painful experiences in your life.

Violence is experienced as a validation of our belief that there are dangerous external forces that we need to be protected from. To realize that you chose an abusive experience does not diminish how painful it was. What it does do, is allow you to realize that as it was you that once chose it, you may also un-choose it. Violence flows from the belief in the validity of violence. By identifying and releasing your beliefs around the need for violence, you can live without violence. Depending on how you choose to define a problem, violence can be seen as a solution, but it is never the only solution. Open your heart to see how your reality can be without violence.

The idea that we choose our own abuse is painful, because it asks us to open up and integrate the pain we are carrying in our wounds. To heal your wounds you must let down the walls around them such that you can reach them, but to heal a wound is to experience the pain it holds as it leaves you. Taking responsibility for your wounds is to empower yourself to heal them. These can be painful words to hear, but the purpose of these words is not to cause pain, it is to help feed the choice to free the pain that is held in this world through the belief in violation.

The journey of healing a wound will take you through many emotions. The realization that violation is a choice does not invalidate anger at your abuser. It does not excuse abuse. If anger is what you feel, allow it. That is what allowance of your being is – allow yourself to feel whatever you feel. To say you chose your own abuse, is not to say that you are to 'blame' for it; there is no blame in self-responsibility; it is only to say that at one time you were in a lot of pain. The final stage of healing is forgiveness of both yourself and your abuser. There is no action that you are not capable of forgiving; there is no wound that you cannot heal. The reason forgiveness is necessary is not moral. It is because if you do not forgive your abuser, then you are in denial of your unity with all life, which includes them. Lack of forgiveness, which can be experienced through many different emotions, is a feeling of separation between you and your abuser. It is a literal wedge of energy created by a belief that they are different from you – that difference being encapsulated in whatever emotive words you would use to describe them.

The reason we create the pain of another person abusing us into our life is not to cause us pain, but to show us that we are already in pain through beliefs we are holding about ourselves and the nature of reality. It could be the manifestation of our feeling of worthlessness, powerlessness, or disgust at our self. It could be out of guilt and shame through which we believe we deserve to be punished. It may simply be the belief that humanity is abusive by nature. There can be many diverse reasons. What ties these reasons together is that they are all masking a feeling of pain that is then manifest in the pain of the abuse. The abuse (not the abuser) is then a teacher. It gives us an external symbol of a wound we carry that we are not acknowledging internally. We can then work to heal that wound through its external manifestation. The form the wound takes, and the journey we must travel to release it from our lives, is the undoing of the beliefs that created it. To leave abuse, which is to release it, is to heal a wound.

There is no abuse that you are meant to endure. There is no lesson that requires you to stay in an abusive situation. The lesson of abuse is always to take back your power, such that you release the pain from your life. Usually this involves releasing the abuser from your life. When someone demonstrates who they are choosing to be in this lifetime through abusive words or actions, believe them. Feel the energy of their being and decide if you want that feeling in your life.

You do not need to punish your abusers. If you want to release what they represent from your life then forgive them. Forgive them so you can let them go. The greatest gift of love you can give to an abuser is to cease to accept their abuse and release them from your life. Take responsibility for the people you have in your life; it is only ever you that is allowing them to be there. Be with people that make you feel good about being who you are.

Unfolding 20
You Cause What Affects You

The perception of time being linear has become as integral to our experience of reality as the solidity of matter. The fluidity of reality that you are awakening to not only includes synchronicity, but also coming to perceive time in a more fluid way. Past and future are powerful ideas that we use to separate our experience. We have determined that the past is unalterable from the present, and that the present cannot be affected by the future. In this way we perceive the unfolding of our experience in a linear fashion from the belief that what is ahead on the timeline cannot affect what is behind it. This creates the arrow of time and, like the whole of our reality system, it is a product of our perception.

To organize experience in this way has been incredibly helpful. Just as to awaken to the illusion is not to dissolve physicality, after awakening we remain in a form of linear time; however, our experience of time does become more fluid. This fluidity is reflected in the loosening of its linearity. A good example of this comes from examining the assumption of cause and effect, as this is the basis for the way in which we apply linearity to our thinking.

Typically we see our emotional state as being the result of what we are experiencing in our reality. If situations we perceive as negative are happening we feel depressed, or maybe angry. If good things are happening we feel happy and positive. Through the idea of cause and effect, reality is seen as being the *cause* of our mood. This is to believe that reality is not only separate from us, but also determines our state of beingness – an expression of being a slave to reality.

To see through the illusion that reality is separate from you is to see through the idea of cause and effect. If you are one with reality then it cannot *cause* you to feel – it *is* your feeling. To integrate this idea is to see reality as the expression, rather than the cause, of what you are feeling. This is to remove time from the equation. For example, if something happens that makes you feel angry, rather than seeing your anger as the result of the event, see the event as being the expression of anger that you were already feeling. You brought yourself to the event in order to feel the anger, thereby releasing it. You freely participated in the event because it was a vehicle to outwardly express something you were feeling.

Without a belief in cause and effect you can no longer deny responsibility by blaming external events or people for your emotional state. No person or thing *makes* you feel anything. You choose to allow the experience of all that affects you emotionally. The idea of cause and effect is a symbol of the separation of our being over time. It is a way in which we simplify and make sense of the world. To let go of linearity is to bring great clarity into your life. It is to see that all experiences that you participate in are a choice. This brings into focus how you are responsible for your own life because it is you that chooses it.

Letting go of the idea of cause and effect will trigger many resistances. These will be walls that you created through blaming external forces for both your emotional state and the condition of your reality. To take complete responsibility for your creatorship is to release the idea of blame, and stand in the acknowledgement that nothing is limiting you but yourself. All the limits in your reality are but a reflection of ways in which you believe you are limited.

In seeing that we cause what affects us, we are also stripped of the feeling of being justified in retaliation. Imagine that I decide to hit you, and you decide to hit me back. This energetic event is two people hitting each other – that is the exchange. However the tendency is to use cause and effect to feel justified in your retaliation. This is a denial that you are the creator of your own reality and thereby, on some level, you gave permission to be hit. If your response was to hit me back then that would be a part of the reason you gave permission. In clarity, the exchange would simply be to acknowledge that we wanted to hit each other and get on with it without the blame. To apply this to your life is to take any situation as a complete energetic exchange with no regard for its sequence. This is to see the exchange as being agreed upon by your Godself before it was played out into reality.

Our belief in linear time creates a wall of resistance to our perception of the future. We each have a host of what are felt as intuitive senses which have the ability to perceive across time. This is not magic. Our Godself, the unified awareness of *All That We Are*, is not contained within the illusion of duality, of which time is an aspect. To awaken out of the illusion of duality is therefore to allow yourself to acknowledge the constant stream of information that comes to you from these inner senses – from your Godself. This is experienced as coming to validate your intuition as a credible source of guidance.

We are surrounded by an ocean of unfolding potentials. As we interact with these potentials we are unfolding our co-created experience with them. By focusing on a potential we begin to integrate with it and it emerges into our reality – the realization of our consciousness. At this point it becomes externally visible, sometimes on the distant horizon, such as a choice of a trip we could take in the future, or immediately, such as bumping into a friend. This is when we have allowed ourselves to become conscious of the potential, leading it to tangibly unfold before us. We have however been interacting with the event, from the level of our Godself, prior to its manifestation. How conscious we are of this is determined through our beliefs as to whether or not this is possible. If you do not believe in foresight then you will not experience it. In the above examples, someone open to feeling their Godself may have started to pick up synchronicities about the destination for the trip, or may have had a feeling they were going to see their friend that day.

The more you are willing to loosen your beliefs about the limits of time, most notably in regards to the ability to feel potential events unfolding before they occur, the more expanded the horizon of your perception will become. The future is not written; it is potential. It is a landscape that is unfolding before you; with every choice that you make, it changes. You choose which energetic events are brought into your reality through your interaction with this landscape of potentials. Your beliefs determine how you traverse the terrain and what enters into your reality – is actualized. Once something becomes visible in your reality you then start interacting with it consciously. Therefore, by coming to expand the limits of your perception, by giving validity to your intuition, you will be able to give your conscious choice to potential energetic events when they are further away from your immediate reality. This is experienced as reality becoming more aligned with what you are consciously desiring – the experience of being more unified with your reality.

Intuition is a direct experience and not something mystical. It is to be open to perceiving feelings from your heart as directly as you perceive light through your eyes. Only you can choose to give validity to your intuition. The more you let your feelings be a factor in your choices, the more you will see the power of their guidance. The more validity you give them, the stronger and clearer they will become. The strength of your intuitions is a reflection of your belief in them. Allow yourself the freedom of feeling the potentials of your unfolding. Allow yourself the freedom inherent in living through your heart.

Unfolding 21
Shields Are Wounds

To be in allowance of *all* experience is to be in the unfolding. Through attachment to our life being a set way, we potentially bring ourselves to experience pain through our resistance to the unfolding. We experience the pain as coming from the event we are resisting, meaning that we label the event as painful, rather than seeing that it is our resistance to it that is creating the pain. This pain can be experienced in many diverse ways such as grief, fear, guilt, physical pain, or loneliness.

Pain in itself adds much color and contrast to life. To wish to never experience pain is to wish not to have been born into this type of physical reality. Pain does not need to be feared. To fear pain is to reject a part of beingness – a part of yourself. Fear of pain will only ever lead you to pain, for it is to doubt your Godhood. Pain is fundamentally no more than a sensation, and is neither inherently positive nor negative, this is a judgment that we apply to it. To see this is to see the difference between pain and suffering.

Pain is of the moment, when the energy of an experience moves through your being. It is our acute fear of pain that creates most of what we perceive as its negative aspects. The fear of what a pain could be is usually worse than the reality. When experienced as a choice, such as getting a tattoo or watching an upsetting movie, and without the preconception that it will be negative, pain can be felt purely as a concentration of stimulation. As such its intensity can even become perceived as being pleasurable. Even a painful emotional experience has its own beauty in the feeling of aliveness that rides on the waves of emotion that flow from it; a good cry can feel wonderful. The purpose of pain is not to hurt us; it is a *signal* to focus us on resistance in our being. A physical wound hurts simply to alert us that it needs to be tended to; this is to help us, not hurt us.

When we experience pain at a level where we come to fear for an aspect of our being, we seek to shut it down – reject it from our consciousness. We do this by building a wall of resistance between it and our conscious perception of it. The area of pain becomes cocooned in our resistance and we are shielded from it. Instead of the pain being experienced and released, it becomes trapped in our being; carried forward with us as a wound. A wound is an energetic event that was felt to be too painful to be completely experienced when it occurred. Any aspect of it which we could not accept is stored in order to be processed later. Until we feel able to deal with it, we carry it as a wound. The wound then becomes a part of our story because it becomes a boundary in our being – a line we will not cross out of fear of re-experiencing what we were feeling when the wound was created.

A wound can be seen as pain elongated over time through our resistance to experiencing it; this is suffering. Pain is not suffering unless we make it so through our resistance to feeling it. Pain is an acutely intense moment and once that moment is past, if we allow ourselves to feel it, then it is gone. It is not possible to experience pain through memory. You can of course remember that you felt pain, but the actual experience of the pain is not something that can be laid down in memory. If in remembering a painful event you feel the pain directly, it is because that pain is still with you in the form of a wound. You are not remembering it; you are still experiencing it. Though not pleasant, wounds are not a mistake or failure. They are a mechanism we use to process experience at a rate we can cope with. They are a way in which we can choose to express and define our story.

The boundary of a wound (the resistance which surrounds the pain) is experienced as being a shield. In the original painful experience, the desire to shield ourselves from that pain creates a shield. If in the future we start getting close to the pain, then the shield is experienced instead of the pain. This is a self-protective instinct, but it is also an instinct that serves to maintain our wounds. The shield is in fact a statement of belief that what we are being shielded from is dangerous, will hurt us, or will perhaps even destroy us. Though shields are something that we associate with keeping us safe, they are in fact a statement of a belief in danger. You only need protection if you fear there is danger. A shield is a fear. A fear is something that repels us away from experience.

The linear view of being wounded is that an external event occurs that causes a wound. Out of the experience of that hurt we create a shield to protect ourselves and prevent that hurt being experienced again. The event that caused the wound is then seen as the cause of the shield. The creation of the shield is seen as the effect of the painful event. This is a denial of our creatorship, in the form of our denial that we are the cause of the pain. We deny ourselves as being the source and, in not seeing the painful event as a reflection of us, we are forced to conclude that it was an external dangerous force that hurt us. This results in the creation of a belief in danger which is manifested as a shield being created. The shield seeks to partition off the painful area of being. That area of being can then be seen to be a part of our own being that we are suppressing. A wound is the rejection of a part of our own being – a part that we perceive as too painful to deal with.

To make sense of this partitioned off area we then apply a descriptive label to the shield in order to justify it. These labels are our fears and in essence read: "Do not go beyond this point. There is pain here. You do not need what is here. It will hurt you." This message is more than a warning; it is the energy of fear. To experience one of your shields is to feel fear. To awaken is to change these labels to: "Beyond this point lies a part of yourself that, at the time this shield was created, you did not feel you could handle. When you feel you are ready, come back here and lower this shield to integrate this part of your being and release yourself from the fear it represents." This is to see without the illusion of cause and effect, through to a singular energetic event where you closed down a part of your being – a contraction of being through the creation of a fear. The belief in the danger and the shield are one – two sides of the same energetic event. The perception of the danger and the raising of the shield are one. They create each other. There is no danger except that which is created by shields. A shield is a belief in danger.

To heal a wound is to face a fear, put down a shield, and allow the experience you originally denied to pass through your being. In releasing a wound you will therefore feel its pain, but instead of holding it to you through resistance, you release it by accepting the message you could not originally accept. Though you will still feel the energy that you originally labeled as painful, it can now be felt as liberation, for to heal a wound is to step out of a cage. Though it may still be painful, it will not be the same as when you originally sealed it up because you have changed, and you will bring your new clarity to it. Some wounds can be so old that when we open them to be healed we do not feel any pain at all. This is not because the energy has gone, but because we are at a point where we do not perceive that energy as painful, even though originally it was painful enough to wound us.

Can you believe that there is nothing in reality that you need to shield yourself from? Can you release your belief in danger? Shields only ever shield you from one thing; the realization that you are safe.

Unfolding 22
You Do Not Know What You Fear

Our being is limitless. It is free. There is no external force that limits who you are or where you can go. The reasons why we limit ourselves are all meaningful and well chosen. It is through these choices that we explore and unfold the realization of our being. To truly experience limiting ourselves we had to forget that it was a choice that we were making. Without this forgetting we would have remained in contact with our unity to all things and the safety of what we are. We would not have experienced the depths of the illusion of separation from which so much has birthed. By nature we like to challenge ourselves; this is why we came here.

What was needed was a way of separating aspects of being such that we could experience being individuated. How could we stop ourselves as limitless beings using that complete freedom? What was needed was a feeling that could be associated with whatever aspect we wanted to separate from, such that when we felt that feeling we backed out of that area of being – something that could be the energetic equivalent of a physical barrier. The feeling that we created through this intention is what we now experience as fear.

There is nothing that limits you but your own fear. All that appears to limit you is but a manifestation of your fear. All fear is a wound as it represents shutting off of an aspect of *all* being from the experience of your *individuated* being. Any wound that we bear creates events that reveal it to us in different lights and from different angles. Wounds are reflected in our reality by manifesting in any situation to which they relate. This is the basis of repeating patterns in life. It is the energy of our wounds expressing themselves as they seek resolution. This is a part of the motion of the unfolding. That which is wounded seeks its release through healing. Aspects of your being that you have shut off from your consciousness seek to be re-integrated. All consciousness seeks wholeness.

Wounds are the illusion that you are not whole. You are whole. The unfolding is the motion towards this realization. The unfolding naturally reveals that what you have separated from is a part of you. It leads us to the realization that what we believe is not us, is us, for we are all; we are God. All that you fear is you – a part of your being you are rejecting. The only thing you ever fear is yourself – the realization of *All That You Are*. All that is outside you is a reflection of you. There is nothing you need to fear. There are many experiences, such as violation, that I would not recommend, but this does not mean that they need to be feared.

Fear is a tool used to create our sense of definition. It is the tool we have used to separate being through the experience of duality that it creates. The scale of love-fear is the closest expression we have of the base polarity from which all others stem. It is the perception through which we can *separate* self from other, and it is the perception through which we can *unify* self and other. To release this polarity, and see through duality, is to see that there is nothing to fear. All that you experience is the manifestation of your own being. There is nothing out there but an infinitely unfolding reflection of you – of God.

Your mind tells you that you understand what it is that you fear through the label you attach to it – the definition you have written on the shield which represents the fear. The definition says something like: "I fear being left. I fear being hurt. I fear having my heart broken. I fear getting my hopes up. I fear losing my money. I fear being attacked. I fear death." However, by definition, you do not know what you fear. All fears are self-created illusions. All fears are meaningful delusions, through which we define and express our story.

To fear something is to have separated yourself from it. If you knew what you have separated yourself from (and to know something is to see it with clarity) then you would know it is you (you would experience your unity with it) and you would therefore not fear it. To know something is to not fear it. Anything that you know, you cannot fear, as to know it is to see that it is you. To know you are God is to not fear what you are. Therefore, you do not know what you fear: *that is how you can fear it.* All fear is of the unknown; that is a definition for fear. Fear causes us to not see what we fear clearly, hence it is not known, and hence it is feared. Fear is that which clouds; it is the opposite of clarity.

A fear is a belief in the danger that will erupt if its shield is let down – if the fear is faced. Shields are the definition of a fear – the boundary that defines a wound. A fear is what you came up with to convince yourself to keep an area of your being shut down. Fears are not real because they deny that what is being shut down is a part of you. They are real in that reality reflects your beliefs to you and the walls of your fears are beliefs. This is the conundrum. Fear is self-enforcing. Through your belief in the validity of a fear you create experiences that confirm it. To be free of a fear is to see through the illusion of it. Sometimes this can be to directly realize it is not true, and see that what lies on the other side of its shield is part of your being – a part of your freedom. At other times it can be that you become so frustrated by the limitation of a fear that you are willing to accept what you fear happening in order to be free of it. Either way the action is the same. It is to cease to resist what you fear. It is to cease trying to stop what you fear happening. It is to cease blocking the unfolding and that is to let what will be, be.

To step into a fear is to step into one of your barriers. It is to cease to let the barrier be a barrier to your consciousness. It is to bring your awareness to an area that you previously feared experiencing. This is the allowance of your being – the allowance of vulnerability. It is to step back into nakedness, for it is to put down a shield. It is to drop the fig leaf and step back into the freedom that Eden represents.

Allowance of this feeling of vulnerability will transform fear into strength. It is to see that to allow yourself to be vulnerable is to be strong, and that to feel the need to bare physical strength is to fear being vulnerable. This is to see through a polarity – to see the strength in being vulnerable. It is to see how the two ends of the polarity are the same. It takes the greatest strength to allow yourself to be defenseless. It is to see that all shields are weapons and that all weapons are fear – defense is attack. The feeling of strength in vulnerability is the returning of the part of your being that you were separated from within the illusion. It is to return to an aspect of your freedom – to step out of a cage.

To allow vulnerability is to realize you are invulnerable, as it is to be without fear. Suffering comes through fear. Without fear in your being, to give suffering a foothold, you will experience safety. The allowance of vulnerability is to step into your fear. When you step into your fear you release it, for only one of two things can happen; either what you fear does not happen, and you realize it was unfounded, or what you were fearing does happen, and you realize that not only can you cope with it but it is the healing of a wound, and you are liberated. Either way the fear is released. Either way you experience more of the freedom that you are.

Put down your shields to heal your wounds. Face your fears to realize that there is no danger 'out there'. There is only you and you are love. You do not know what you fear. The only way to truly discover what you fear is to go into it. It is not wrong to fear. Fear is but the choice to deny your own freedom.

Unfolding 23
Judgment is a Cage

To face a fear is to see that a belief you are carrying is limiting you and is therefore on some level causing you pain. To face and release this fear is to recognize the core belief that was taken on in its formation. The fear and the belief are one. It is as true to say that the fear flows from the belief, as it is to say that the belief is the ideological representation of the fear. To release one is to release the other. The belief, the fear, and all their manifestations such as pain, alienation, separation, and limitation, are all different faces of the cage of a wound. By working to release any one face, so all the others are stimulated and released. The definitions of our stories can become extremely intricate. However the wounds which that complexity masks tend to be rudimentary hurts such as abandonment and shame.

Wounds flow from pain. Pain flows from fear. Fear flows from the illusion of separation. Separation is created by resistance. Resistance flows from belief. Only with a belief in separation can you experience something external hurting you. This separation is a product of duality – the polarities of belief with which we divide being. The division of duality separates you from the realization of your wholeness. That which we seek is only ever a reflection of an aspect of our being that we have become separated from. This internal division is a wound. To heal a wound is to see clearly the belief in separation that the wound is founded on; this belief is discovered to be a judgment. A judgmental belief states that one end of a polarity is superior to the other end. Judgmental beliefs cause you to separate from an aspect of your being, because all that you judge is only ever a reflection of an aspect of yourself. All judgments, all hate, is of the self.

To have judgmental beliefs is to give away your power of choice to those judgments. Instead of choosing from your heart, your choices instead come from your judgments. These then dictate how you *should* act, who you *should* favor, and what it is you *should* strive to be. The basis of judgmental beliefs is the belief in the fundamental separation that we call right and wrong, also seen as good and evil. This separation creates righteousness – the moral justification to act with cruelty. Our greatest atrocities have come from the belief in acting for the "greater good". The belief in right and wrong, more than any other belief, creates the belief in absolutes – such as a belief that a particular action is always wrong. To believe in absolutes is a denial that everything changes. Change is the greatest constant. One of the beautiful aspects of the unfolding is that, in its constant flow of change, all absolute beliefs are eventually released. This frees us from getting stuck indefinitely in any singular belief. It continually moves us towards the realization that we are the creators of our belief.

A judgment is essentially a declaration of separation. It is a rejection of a part of yourself. To judge is to be caught in the illusion of separation, and the perception of that separation as being superior. It is to lose sight of the equality of all being. Judgment is a statement of being in pain. Anyone who expresses prejudice is saying that they are in pain and fear – they are wounded. What they are prejudiced against is a symbol of a part of themselves that they are rejecting. The argument a person gives as to why they are prejudiced reveals in its description the polarities which they are in conflict with.

For example, someone who is homophobic, who believes that being gay is unnatural, is having an issue with an aspect of their own being that they judge as unnatural. This person filters their world view through a polarity of natural-unnatural, with a belief that what they *choose* to label as unnatural is in some way inferior or defective. Similarly, a homophobic man that focuses his prejudice on effeminacy would most commonly be in rejection of his own feminine energy. This would be someone that judges the feminine to be inferior to the masculine. In both these examples the action is the same; it is to divide the worth of beingness through polarity, by assigning superiority to one end of the scale and inferiority to the other. This is the action of segregation, not only of the external world, but also of the persons own internal beingness. All beingness that is seen as being at the 'negative' end of the scale is suppressed, an aspect of being is denied validity, and that denial is manifested as limitation. When we judge others, the only person that we limit is ourselves.

To release a judgment is to see the equality of both ends of a polarity. This does not mean that the ends are identical. It is that they are of equal worth – equal validity. They are not better or worse than each other, just different. To release judgment, see the pros and cons of both ends. It is to see that in balance there is equality. To be in allowance is to see that:
o in some situations the feminine energy will be most effective, and in other situations it will be the masculine.
o limitation can produce some wonderful experiences of being. Limitation and is not inferior to freedom.
o sometimes the extremes at either end of a polarity are not necessarily the most joyful experience – more is not necessarily better. The middle way often leads to the greatest freedom.

o nothing in life is inherently bad. It is our choice of perception that creates this judgment.

o if we have wounds, then more money will not resolve them. Our wounds will always be expressed.

o superiority is just a way in which we cage ourselves out of fear of intimacy. Inferiority is a cage in just the same way.

o you are better than no one, and no one is better than you. You are second to none.

To release judgment is to let go of hierarchy and morality. It is to let go of law and control. Breathe the freedom of equality and truly taste the world for what it is, rather than through your judgment of how you believe it should be. See the world through the eyes of equality and you will see it at its most beautiful – *as it is*.

Judgment is a way in which we organize our view of the world, a way of prioritizing what we do and do not want to interact with – where we do and do not feel safe. It is both effective and efficient in preserving a singular, rigid story. Judgment has served us well in our exploration of separation. It has allowed us to create defined groups in which we have explored certain areas of being with great focus. It has allowed us to focus inside of ourselves, through the feeling of safety engendered by identifying with others who share our prejudices. Judgment has been a vessel for exploring alienation, rejection, hatred, bigotry, and elitism. By understanding these we better understand unity, allowance, love, acceptance, and equality. Judgment has done exactly what we asked it to do. It is important to see its validity in the world in order to release it. You cannot release being judgmental whilst you remain in judgment of it.

The experience of judgment is the meat of resistance. It is the substance that fills the space of separation that resistance creates. Your judgment of reality stands between you and the world. Instead of perceiving directly 'what is', you see reality only after you have applied your judgment to it – distorting it with the separatism of your fear. To be free of judgment is to see the equality of being. It is to see reality with clarity, and that is to see yourself with clarity.

Once free of prejudice, you enter a world of choice and preference. Bring your heart to reality so that you can *feel* life instead of have your mind separate you from it. Cease to judge your own being such that you can freely and fearlessly *be* whatever you feel to be.

Unfolding 24
To Create is Not to Control

In the realization that you are the creator of your reality it is seen that even though your reality flows from you, this does not mean that you control it. Creation is not an act of control. The energy of seeking to control something is a rejection of creation. No element of your reality requires your control. To believe in the need for control is to be blind to the beauty of the unfolding. It is to believe that without your effort reality will be inferior. What you create has its own form of consciousness; to seek to control it is no different than seeking to control another human being.

When you first step into your power of creation there is little doubt that there will be much you will want to change about your reality. It is our nature to look to remove what we do not want, before we start to create what we do want. To desire new things in your reality is not in itself a desire to control. It is through your implementation of this desire that control can arise. What distinguishes creation from control is whether the expression of your desire is founded on the allowance, or the rejection, of your reality. Control is an act of rejection. Creation flows from allowance.

When you express your desire as control, you effectively want to destroy an aspect of your reality. The energy of that rejection is one of judgment; a judgment that states your desire to separate from that aspect of 'what is'. In essence you are seeking to reject it even though, as a part of your reality that you are responding to, it is a reflection of your being. To reject something in this way is to judge that there is something 'wrong' with it. It is to deny that it, in some way, represents you. Control, in its energy of rejection, is a mechanism of separation.

What you are rejecting is either seen as something external to be pushed away, or as something that is deficient within you that it is best to suppress. This is a denial that it is of your own creation – of you. Whatever you seek to reject has not hurt you; it has only ever been an *expression* of your pain, and that pain has only ever been from your rejection of that part of yourself. It is circular. There is no cause and effect in choosing from the heart. To reject something is to believe that you will feel better by destroying its existence in your reality, but what you are rejecting is not your pain. The act of rejection is the pain.

Do not reject what you want to change in your life. Acknowledge that it is an aspect of you which has served you in coming to see yourself, even if this experience was painful. It has been a gift because it has led you to see an aspect of your being that you were rejecting.

Pain is a mechanism that causes you to focus on an aspect of your being that you are separating from, such that the energy of your focus can potentially bring about its reintegration (healing). When you reject your pain, and refuse to see its message, then it becomes suffering. Pain does not need to make you suffer; when pain is seen with clarity it becomes a signpost to your freedom.

To create is to express the energy of love in your being. It is to focus what you *do* want, rather than focus on what you *do not* want. To focus on what you do want is to *feel* the joy of it in your being. It is to *love* what you want, thereby attracting it to you. To focus on rejecting what you do not want is to create ties of identification that hold it to you. Your focus on it only brings it closer. The statements "I am" and "I am not" are both statements of identification; in this context the 'not' is irrelevant. Whatever you focus upon you pull into your reality, whether your focus is one of love or rejection. This is how we come to create what we fear. Our fear acts as a focus that causes what we fear to manifest. So rather than trying to control 'what is', simply allow it to be, and focus on what you do want. To allow your reality is to release your attempts to control it. When you do this, the loving, attractive energies of your desire will bring about what you do want.

Letting go of the energy of rejection is a gradual journey. It is to release an ingrained way of being. Years of living with something you hate creates many bonds with that thing. Anger, hate, and rejection are strong forces of identification. Any emotion is a force of attraction. To feel emotion about something is to draw it to you. The fact that it is stimulating emotion in you means that it carries a message for you. The very emotion is the message. Only in allowing yourself to feel the emotion will you hear the message. When you have heard and integrated the message, and therefore the emotion, you will have released your focus on it from your reality.

The opposite of love is the opposite of anger; it is indifference. True indifference to something is an absence of emotional response. As such it represents an absence of desire to control that thing. This is the complete allowance of it to be as it is. To be indifferent to something is to release that thing from your reality because you are no longer associating your identity with it, or acting to dissociate your identity from it. This is to allow it to be as it is – to go on its way. Indifference is to neither pull something towards you, nor push it away. This makes indifference an effortless state. You cannot force yourself to be indifferent. You cannot *work* towards being indifferent about something you are trying to release from your life. You cannot force yourself to feel nothing – to do so is to go into a form of self-numbing which is to suppress (reject) your emotions. Indifference for something cannot be manufactured; it only arises from coming to accept it as it is. This is to come into balance and integration with it.

To release something from your life that you have been trying to reject, open yourself up to accept it. This does not mean you have to enjoy its presence. It is to accept its existence in your reality such that you are ceasing to reject it. This is to realize and acknowledge that it has been a *valid* part of the expression of your being. It is to allow the idea that it can remain in your reality, and however long it remains will be meaningful. It is to know that when it leaves your reality will be when it has served its purpose and delivered its message to you. If you release the control of rejecting what you do not want, and focus positively on what you do want, you will be allowing the harmony of the unfolding into your reality.

Creation is an act of love – love for your being, love of life, and love of love. It is a journey of exploration through birthing new and exciting experiences into your reality, rather than seeking to manipulate and control what is already there. It is to realize that what is before you is beautiful because it is reflecting you to yourself, and you are beautiful; even when you are exploring aspects of being such as separation, pain, or control. Rejecting an aspect of your reality will intensify rather than release it. To accept your reality is to allow it to flow – to change. To be in the flow of life is neither to seek to hold an experience to you, nor push it away. It is simply to *be* in the experience. This is to be in the *Now*.

The reality before you is the most meaningful experience you could be having in this moment. It is never a mistake. To become aware of its message of love, you must allow the experience of your reality into yourself. This is to be one with it, rather than to reject, resist, or judge it. This is to experience it with clarity. It is to hear its message, which is to allow it to transform into the next experience. Hear the message of your current reality in order to release its rigidity, such that your fluid dreams can unfold

Unfolding 25
You Are Perfectly Abundant

Our level of abundance is one of the primary ways in which we express ourselves. To be abundant is to express your connection with the innate freedom of your being. The experience of lack is an expression of a feeling of limitation and isolation. Allowing your abundance is central to feeling your inner power, both to be free within the world and to affect the world. Money and abundance, though often linked, are not directly related. Money in itself is not freedom, and can even become a cage. Abundance refers to a bountiful flowing of energy that can be manifest in such ways as money, support, synchronicities, and love. When flowing from abundance, these aspects of being represent a great freedom to do whatever you want to do, and be who you want to be. As such they also represent the potential for great change.

A belief in lack, whether it is a lack of money, freedom, or love is a way in which we define our stories. We often talk of all the things we would do if only we were abundant. We use lack as a logical justification as to why we are not living our dream, why we are staying in a situation that is unfulfilling, or why we are not happy. A focus on lack can quickly become an extremely powerful part of a person's definition. As miserable as we may feel that lack is, it also helps keep our life static and cozy. Lack keeps fear of the unknown (of uncontrolled change) at bay. Misery can be extremely comfortable.

Opening the flow of your abundance, when it has been used to keep you in a safe space, is therefore extremely threatening to your story. It is to lift your foot from the brake and let in all the changes you have been resisting through a belief that your lack made them not possible. A belief in lack is resistance to those changes that an allowance of abundance will bring. The unfolding and abundance are inseparable; both symbols of flow and change. They are rivers whose currents cannot be controlled. To allow them into your life is to realize that they are safe, even though you cannot control them.

One common barrier to trusting yourself with abundance comes from previously using the empowerment of abundance in destructive ways. The freedom that abundance can bring into your life will empower you to do what you want; as such it will amplify the polarity of your story. Not only will areas where you create joy magnify, so too will areas where you create suffering. Lack of abundance is one way that people with addictions control this aspect of their being. With complete freedom of abundance, the ability to destroy your story becomes more immediate. What this highlights is that lack of abundance is not a mistake — it is meaningful. Your level of abundance is a message to you. If you will allow yourself to hear that message you will be letting in the change that it represents. Your abundance will be a carrier of the change you are resisting.

To hear the message is to realize the ways in which your lack of abundance has been serving you. To see this is to cease to reject your experiences of lack. It is to realize that even poverty is not a mistake; it has not been trying to hurt you; you have chosen it because it has been serving your story in some way. It may have been protecting you from your self-destructive tendencies, or from quitting a job and becoming isolated. Poverty may have been an excuse to keep you from having to face your fears, or face the reality of making your dream happen. It may have been artificially tying you to someone you are afraid to leave. It may have been keeping you working long hours because you do not want to face life at home. It may be a direct reflection of a feeling of worthlessness that leads you to see your worth. It may simply be showing you that you believe poverty is the natural state. Whatever the reason you have been creating it through the reflection of your beliefs.

Hear the message of your state of lack to release your reality into transformation, such that your abundance can come in. Know that it will change your reality in ways you cannot control. Often people ask for their reality to stay roughly the same, except with more money. Abundance is not a flow that can be controlled in this way. Control shuts down abundance. Abundance cannot come into your life in a controlled form. Abundance is freedom; control seeks to suppress freedom. To have a list of things you want to change and a list that you want to stay the same, will not work. Money will change your life in ways you do not expect. It is not an energy that you can predict or predetermine. It will bring new things into your life and it will cause others to leave. Abundance is uncontrollable change, pure and simple. Realize the difference between wanting change and needing change. If you desire abundance then open yourself to change without seeking to define how it will come or how it will affect you. Feel it as the energy of change, empowerment, and freedom. Feel this in your being to release your control and allow your innate abundance to manifest.

Like the unfolding, abundance is a state of letting go of how you define yourself and your reality. To feel abundance is to feel the bounty of the energy of your own being. Abundance is not an external state of wealth; it is an internal realization of your own limitlessness.

To feel abundance in your being is to have it reflected externally in your reality. Whilst having abundance flow through your reality, you cannot remain meek, unassuming, or unworthy. To allow abundance is to allow the realization of your own magnificence to flow through your being. All that you seek to be, comes from this flow within you. Reality cannot make you happy. Reality can only reflect your own happiness to you. Feel your own value internally to see yourself valued in the world. You assign your own worth.

To allow this realization of abundance into your being and have it flow out into manifestation, let go of your identification with lack. Whilst you are in a rejection of poverty you hold yourself in it. To reject it is to deny that it has, on some level, been serving you. All lack points to the realization of abundance. Use the message of your lack to discover your abundance. Abundance is not a rejection of poverty. Poverty is a rejection of your natural state of abundance. You cannot control your way out of poverty.

Any wealth built with control has no foundation and requires constant effort in order to maintain it. It will always be surrounded by the fear of losing it. True abundance flows with such ease that there is no fear of losing it. The challenge of abundance is only how much will you let yourself have. How strong can you tolerate its flow of change in your life? How much transformation, freedom, and love can you allow? How much of your story are you willing to let go of?

To allow abundance into your life, allow the realization that your current level of abundance is meaningful. In seeing that it is meaningful you will be giving yourself the clarity of seeing why it is perfect. This will reveal to you the way in which you have been resisting abundance. If you are willing to face the fear that the resistance represents, you will open your reality to change. This is to release identification with lack and limitation. Allow the flow of abundance to come from within you. Feel the power and magnificence of your own being – the boundlessness of your energy. Allow this magnificence to be reflected in your reality without expectation or control. Release it to create freely in the unfolding of your being. You have the right to affect the world. You have the right to change the world. Allow the realization of your significance.

Abundance is not something that is determined externally through your wealth. You are your abundance. Abundance is the realization of your freedom.

Unfolding 26
Wholeness Through Healing

To let go of trying to control your reality is to free yourself to be yourself. Whether your attempt to control flows from trying to change reality into what you think it should be, or from trying to keep it the same, that control is manifested in effort and struggle. To be in effort is to be identified with the illusion of separation and limitation. It is to be living in a test, where depending on your effort and the choices you make, you will either pass or fail.

Attachment is a form of control where your identity becomes attached to reality being a set way. When it is this defined way, you feel good; when it is not, you feel bad. In this state there is no rest or peace as your mood becomes conditional on external factors. Attachment leads to possessiveness, which is where we seek to forcibly hold things in our reality. This is an expression of the fear of loss. We believe that if we do not hold onto what we are attached to, then it will leave us, and we will be diminished. This is to have identified your story with what you are attached to; therefore losing it becomes feared as a loss of a part of yourself. It is to live in fear.

To attach your identity to external things is an expression of feeling incomplete in what you are. To be free of possessiveness is to know that you are everything. It is to be identified with all equally. When you are wounded then the area of being that you are shielding off is shut off within your being (in the illusion, not within your Godself). You start to experience the loss of that part of your being as something missing in your life, and the wound becomes felt as a hole – a feeling of incompleteness. This may be felt as unease, emptiness, loneliness, or in a sense of feeling alienated from those around you.

There is a natural desire to feel whole, as wholeness is the feeling of your Godself. Because of this desire for completeness, the hole created by a wound becomes a *need* to find what is missing. To resist healing a wound internally is therefore to become compelled to heal it externally. It is to seek to resolve the incompleteness with material experiences that in some way represent the aspect of your being that has become shut off. Though you can obtain partial relief (usually through either self-numbing or distraction) from a wound, there is nothing external that can completely fill an internal hole.

The unrelenting pursuit to resolve the inner feeling of emptiness with external relief is the basis of addiction. To lose what you are attached to is to re-open the feeling of emptiness and incompleteness that the attachment was masking. Avoidance of this emptiness leads to a chase where you are continually trying to fill a hole that cannot ever be truly filled by anything except the healing of the wound. The extreme manifestations of this chase can be in compulsive behavior, self-harming, and the many forms of physical addiction. These are all a chase to feel complete – a running from the pain of emptiness.

Emotional attachment to another person is a form of neediness where your happiness becomes dependant on keeping that person in your life. This is not love; it is an addiction to another person. It is to perpetually live in fear of losing them, and in the struggle to hold them in your life. This fear will either manifest in them leaving or in a co-dependant relationship. Your joy becomes secondary as you externalize the power of your beingness into the person you are attached to. As with all addiction, this comes from the desire for wholeness. The other person provides relief to the feeling of emptiness, to be possessive of them is to maintain a fix.

Though you do have the free-will choice to carry your wounds for an entire lifetime, you can never escape having to heal them eventually. Often we try to convince ourselves that living with the pain of a wound is preferable to going back into it. This is to not see the degree to which the pain of that wound is already manifesting in other ways through the hole it creates. To carry a wound for a lifetime is to go through more pain than could ever be experienced by healing the wound in the *Now*.

There is no wound that you are not strong enough to heal. To heal your wounds is to step into the conscious realization of your wholeness. It is to let go of the chase of attachment and its caging of your freedom to be yourself. It is to step from only being able to offer conditional love, to being able to love unconditionally. In this state, where you no longer seek to forcibly hold your attachments in your reality, what remains is what desires to be there. It is to live in a world where what surrounds you is not there because you have imprisoned it; it is there because it is choosing to be. This is to let the experience of being surrounded by love into your life. It is the realization that you are worthy of that love.

When you release attachment there will be much that will leave your life. These are all things that have run their course and are ready to move on. They are experiences that you were artificially sustaining with your effort. To release attachment is to face reality with clarity and allow it to be what it is, rather than what you were trying to force it to be. Initially this may be painful, but through the allowance of that pain will come freedom from addiction. In revealing a hole that you were artificially filling, you are offered the opportunity to see, and thereby heal, the wound which the hole represents.

Your attachments act as temporary bandages which hold you from seeing your wounds. To let them go is to allow your wounds to breathe, heal, and be reintegrated into your being. Though letting go of your attachments may be painful, it is not the pain of loss, it is the pain that you shut down when the original wound was created. The only loss that ever took place was the loss of the aspect of your being that was shut inside the wound. To let go of your attachments is to regain something, not lose it.

Attachment is a way to not deal with your wounds. It is a way to put your energy into holding reality static, rather than allowing the unfolding. The unfolding inevitably leads you to your wounds so that they can be healed. Attachment takes continual effort and struggle against this motion. It holds you in a feeling of incompleteness. Though you may get a temporary fix through an addiction, you are then quickly chasing after the next fix. As such you are not free from the wound at all, but are in constant servitude to it. Addiction is slavery from within.

To open a wound is to face an unknown change to your story. Through the motion of the unfolding, wounds appear to pull you towards them. As long as you are in fear you will resist this, putting your energy into not being pulled in. The wound does not pull at you to hurt you; the pull is because it contains a part of you. Inside the wound is a part of your beingness that seeks to be whole again, in just the same way you seek your own wholeness. If you will allow yourself to fall into the unknown change of healing a wound, through feeling and releasing its pain, you will find the part of yourself that addiction could never complete. You will find your fulfillment – your sovereignty. Sovereignty is to know you are whole. You are complete unto yourself.

You cannot escape healing your wounds. They are a part of you; your freedom lies within their healing. Through the pain of attachment your wounds are continually present in your life. Allow the healing of your wounds by releasing the attachments with which you have been disguising them.

Unfolding 27
The Allowance of Happiness

Being in this world is an amazing vehicle for experiencing everything from orgasmic joy to sheer desolation. In the game of life we are the players and reality is an ever shifting stage that reflects us. The world does not *cause* you to become happy or sad; it is that which houses your happiness and sadness. To look to the world to make you happy is to give away your own power to make yourself happy. It is to be waiting for something external to fill a hole in your being that is internal. It is to look into a mirror and decide that you will not be happy until your reflection smiles back at you.

Any belief that begins with "I will be happy when..." is not only a statement of unhappiness; it is also a commitment to that discontent. This conditional belief has become a common cornerstone to many of our stories, giving definition to the feeling of unhappiness by identifying it with external factors. If you refuse to address your internal wounds then to be happy requires a constant expense of energy. This is because our wounds are our unhappiness; without healing them, happiness will only ever be conditional on external factors, or experienced through the transitory moment of an addictive fix. Another option is to accept our own unhappiness. A belief like, "I will only be happy when I have more money" comes to give comfort as it frees us from the chase to be happy until we have money. It is a way of giving ourselves permission to sit passively by and take comfort in that passivity.

Being fulfilled is not superior to the chase for fulfillment, or the acceptance of being unfulfilled. Happiness is a choice, not a requirement. Sometimes society can make us feel that we have an obligation to be happy. We often miss how content we can be in a definition of unhappiness. Many people are at their most joyful when they are having a good moan. A part of discovering your own happiness is coming to see with clarity where you derive joy; this may be from experiences that are not traditionally seen as being joyful. No one can define how you should be happy except for you. One aspect of finding peace within, is releasing society's preconceptions of what it is to be happy. Do not let someone else's idea of happiness convince you that you are not happy.

A part of allowance is not judging what constitutes happiness, either in yourself or in others. Do not try to 'fix' what you perceive to be the misery of others. Everyone has their own inviolate free-will; to try and 'save' someone from unhappiness is to disregard their sovereignty, even if it is from a desire for them to be happy. If you make your own happiness conditional on the people around you being happy, then you will never be consistently happy. To feel guilty for being happy when others around you are miserable, serves no one. It is simply a way of denying your own life, vitality, and joy. You are the determinant and catalyst of your own happiness. Joy that flows from *within* you is always with you, no matter what is happening externally. Inner happiness is a choice. Central to this choice is the release of the ways in which you have defined yourself through difficulty, struggle, and hardship. Often we come to wear these definitions as medals of honor, proud to have survived such hells. These medals are a self-identification with that struggle, and therefore lead you to re-create that struggle in ever repeating dramas.

The idea that we want to be happy can be an unfounded assumption. If we truly want to be happy then why do we spend so much time worrying, instead of doing what we enjoy? Why do we stick to the same boring routine, instead of acting upon our dreams? Why do we see the worst in situations, instead of the best? Why do we keep making financial choices that keep us in poverty? The way to know if you want to be happy is to look at the choices you are making in your life to see if they reflect the desire to create happiness. This is not about coming to judge yourself; it is about coming to see yourself with honesty and clarity – coming to see what you are really doing versus preconceived notions of what you *think* you are doing. What does the way you are living your life tell you about yourself?

Do not use what you discover to beat yourself up, use it to connect with the reality of your life so that you can bring refreshed intention to it. That to which we blind ourselves stays the same. Self-blinding is a resistance to seeing, and resistance is a force that holds things static. To discover that you have not been choosing happiness is to see your wounds, and therefore begin their healing.

Unhappiness is the choice to be resigned to living with your wounds; this arises out of a fear of facing them. To see this fear is to realize that you have been afraid of being happy. This usually stems from once being extremely happy and then having that happiness end. The loss of that happiness is then felt to be too painful to re-experience, because it is judged to be more painful than the lack of happiness that followed. It therefore feels easier to remain unhappy. It is to believe that it is better to have never loved, than to have loved and lost. We try to convince ourselves that this is not what we believe, but a closed heart says otherwise.

Situations where we feel we lost our happiness are situations where our happiness was conditional upon external factors. It was the loss of the circumstances we were attached to that led to the fall from happiness and the pain that followed. To awaken to your Godself is to connect with an ever flowing stream of well being. It will not always be experienced as joyful happiness; sometimes it will be a feeling of support at a difficult time, the feeling of not being alone, or simply a stranger that smiles at you when you need it. Fulfillment flows from your love for your own being, and your choice to live with an open heart. This is to create a stable foundation through which to enjoy all the wonderful experiences of the world.

To bring happiness into your life, begin by acknowledging the ways in which you are unhappy and why you may be choosing this. Allow yourself to see the ways in which you fear happiness. This is to see the ways in which you feel it has hurt you in the past. Allow these wounds to surface so that they can heal. See the ways in which it was not happiness that hurt you, but only the loss of your attachments. Allow the idea of being happy back into your life, and let your story change accordingly. At first the idea of choosing happiness may feel like taking a risk – the risk of not finding it, or the risk of finding it and then losing it. Let go of your definitions that are based on fear, self-doubt, misery, or struggle. Identify yourself with inner happiness in whatever way you feel it, and know that this will never leave you. You cannot make others happy but, through your own abundance of happiness, you can show others how they too can open their hearts to being happy if they so choose. Happiness radiates.

Your very being is constantly sending out a message into the world. There is no right or wrong in this message. All that is important is that you are happy with it. The message of your being is your most significant contribution to the world. It is not just an expression of your being; it is a constant stream of energy that touches everything. You have the right to be happy and the right to be unhappy – to struggle or to live in ease. Whatever you choose is both purposeful and perfect. Whatever you choose will be shared with all life. Allow yourself the idea that you do not have to be happy. Do this because it allows you to see that happiness is indeed a choice. Once you know happiness is a choice, then you can choose it if you desire. It comes highly recommended.

Unfolding 28
Being Yourself

The *Now* is full of potentials that you can unfold. These are reflected to you through your reality. The world, elongated across time, is a representation of all the potentials that we have so far explored; its continued unfolding is our playground for exploring the experience of being within differentiation. You are in a shared mass reality that gives form and context to your current lifetime.

Your choice to birth (where, when, and as whom) has given certain parameters to your life. From within incarnation you could view these parameters as limitations, but to feel them through your heart is to know that you chose them with complete freedom and wisdom. This original birth choice is far less limiting than many suppose. A part of embracing and loving your being, is to accept and love that moment of birth choice. It is to experience utter affirmation for the choice you made to be born as you – to experience this lifetime.

You chose to be here to explore being *you* – to create what you experience yourself to be. If you are choosing to awaken then you are here to be *you* remembering that you are God, and to explore *your* unfolding from that realization. As much as you may come to connect with the unity of all life, you are not here to shed your individuality.

Even though you are awakening from being contained within a singular story, to being any story you can imagine, you will remain expressed in some form of definition. To believe that you are here to evolve out of your individuality, is to deny the perfection of your choice to birth here. Ultimately, from the widest perspective, you are the world. You are God, and are connected to all the experience that has ever been. To awaken is to connect with this realization of unity with all being. It is not however to leave being *you* to become all, it is to awaken the all within you. You chose to be here to have the experience of being *you*.

To awaken is to awaken *into* life, not from it. To connect with the unity of all life is not to let go of continuing to create your own personal experience. Awakening is not to become without definition; but it is to change your relationship with definition. Instead of experiencing yourself as confined by boundaries that appear to be of external origin, it is to consciously choose your own boundaries. In awakening, even though you maintain definition, you no longer experience the boundaries of that definition as limitations, because you are unified with your creation of them. This is to experience your limitlessness within definition. It is the realization of the freedom of definition. In this state, boundaries are a choice, instead of a fear or limit; their definition gives rise to a form of experience that excites you. That is why you chose to be here as you.

This realization of what it is to awaken from within embodiment is to connect with the perfection of your birth choice. It is to realize that the boundaries of your being can be joyful if you cease to define them from fear, and instead create them with the love and freedom of your sovereign will. To awaken is to see that elements of your birth choice, that you may have previously perceived as limits, are in fact gifts of definition that shape your experience in a way that has brought you to this moment of awakening.

Before we awaken, the boundaries of our being are experienced as external limits. They are associated with wounds, fears, and resistance. They are the ideas that we have used to feel separate from each other, from the world, and even from our own reality – our beingness. They are the energy that contains and limits us; the medium upon which our fear, pain, and separation are reflected back to us. It is this experience of limitation that can lead people to see the idea of awakening as being to escape from, or transcend, this reality – to see physicality as profane, inferior, or simply not evolved. There is no doubt that the experience of separation within duality is intense. It can be intensely joyful and intensely miserable. What makes it wonderful is the intensity. No other reality system is experienced as being this 'real'. This is the game where you forget you are playing a game. This reality expresses the base level of separation; separation from knowing what you are.

To step into your divinity is to step out of the painful aspects of separation by seeing that separation is an illusion. Separation is the basis of duality. Just as duality contains the potential to live in misery, so it also contains the potential to live within joy. Joy and suffering (heaven and hell) are both places on earth. Neither has any definition beyond love and not love – you and not you. Joy is the expression of your heart. Joy is what you are. Suffering is to completely separate yourself from what you are. Joy is the complete allowance of your being. Suffering is to completely resist your being, and thereby your reality. Joy is acceptance. Suffering is rejection.

Love-fear, joy-suffering, heaven-hell, and unity-separation all reflect 'seeing yourself' and 'not seeing yourself' – seeing that you are the creator versus seeing yourself as a biological system in a battle to survive. We have built in a lifespan such that we continually return to our remembrance of our divinity. To awaken is to remember whilst you are alive. In a sense it is to die whilst you are alive because it is to let go of your individuality as you once knew it, but at the same time it is to discover individuality in a whole new way. How you define your being comes to be from love instead of fear.

Awakening to yourself is the realization of the freedom of your being. It is to let go of trying to define your reality with thoughts that flow from your fears and attachments. It is to step into creating yourself from the feeling in your heart – to feel your being and live in the expression of that feeling. Thinking is founded in definition (separating one thing from another) and can only take you so far. You cannot *think* the realization of your Godhood, you can only *feel* it. Do not fear your being: feel your being.

Awakening is not to reject your mind, but it is to let go of associating your primary identity with it. To awaken is to expand your consciousness to that of your heart – your Godself. It is to drop deeper into your embodiment, deeper into the allowance and acceptance of yourself and the reality that you are in. You cannot see that you are God by rejecting this reality – love it, for it is you, it is God. The realization of God is love. It is to see and create yourself from love. Love is in your heart. Your Godself is in your heart. You are in your heart. To see your being clearly is to see yourself as love. To see your being as love is to feel love. To feel love is to unfold it, the un-definition of your being, into the definition of your reality. You are *your own* realization of freedom.

Embracing your decision to birth here is not just about accepting the conditions you chose for your entry into this shared reality. It is about embracing the very essence of the choice to *be here*. Here is not inferior or profane. Here is the *Now*. Here is where your experience of the *Now* is. Here is where you *are*, and you are God. Here is where you realize you are God. Here is the most wonderful place you could possibly be. How can I know that about you? Because I see that *here is where you are choosing to be*. Here is where you are reading this book, and with these words you are being welcomed into your divinity. This reality is wonderful because *you are here*. Here is *Now*, and *Now* is where everything you have ever wanted happens.

Unfolding 29
Clarity

Discernment is the clarity of choosing from your heart. All choices that flow with clarity from the heart are in harmony with not only your personal unfolding, but also the unfolding of the world. The mind tells us that this is not possible, that we as individuals must at times want things that the world does not. This is logic, and is founded on the idea that we are separate from each other. A unified diversity is the realization of the intimate fusion of the unity of the whole with its expression of diversity. It is the realization into being of each individual choice fitting perfectly with the whole.

To choose from your heart is not to consciously choose for the all. It is to purely feel what your heart desires to experience in your personal reality. To make choices where you are *thinking* of what is best for all is not allowance; it is to control. It is the idea that you could possibly know what is better for other people than themselves. At the core of allowance is respect for all things to be as they are, including their chosen path of unfolding. To think you could know better is, through judgment, to see yourself as separate and superior. See the difference between trying to control people and experiencing the joys of co-creating with others to catalyze the unfolding of all involved. The harmony of a unified diversity flows from all beings choosing from their hearts for themselves.

Love and respect the world by letting it choose for itself. To do this is to free yourself from your own control, as when you are trying to control others that energy is reflected back and experienced in your own reality. To control others is to live within a personal reality that is defined by control. To love and respect the world is to live within the energy of love and respect within your own personal reality.

Coming to choose from your heart, according to what feels best for you, can at first feel selfish. The idea of being selfish is a barrier we have used in our separation from our divinity. The idea of selfishness is the association of shame and guilt with loving yourself. To be controlled by the idea of selfishness is to sacrifice your own joy. It is to be contained by the idea that it is self-indulgent to be joyful. The paradox being that there is no greater service you can do for the world than putting your self first, such that you experience the joy of your being. To live in joy is to ground your divinity and make the whole world more joyful.

The foundation of bringing love to the world starts with loving yourself. Choosing what feels best for you, from your heart, is simultaneously the most selfish and selfless thing you can do. It is to see the illusion of the polarity of selfish-selfless as being a mechanism of control and limitation. To release it is to see through the judgment of self-indulgence. To be selfless is selfish, and to be selfish is selfless. To aid all is to aid yourself. To aid yourself is to aid all.

Beliefs are rarely clear cut. They usually reflect many fragments of experience that may conflict with each other. The motion of the unfolding is to clarify this fragmentation. This clarification occurs through the choices that unfold before you. Many of your choices are symbolic representations of your fragmented beliefs. For example, one experience may have told you that being in love is wonderful, whilst another told you that love was the route to pain. This creates a fragmented belief about being in love. Eventually this will manifest as a choice, with one option symbolizing the choice to see being in love as pleasurable, and the other choice as painful. Whatever perspective you then choose represents the clarification of your belief about being in love. Regardless of how you choose, the fragmentation is resolved.

What is seen here is that clarity does not mean to see through to some transcendent, universal truth; it means to see clearly what you believe. There is no right or wrong to what you believe. The existence of right and wrong itself is simply a belief. To awaken is to come to clearly know what your beliefs are. This is to be consciously aware of the stage from which you create. Your perception of reality can be used as a gauge of this. You are seeing clearly when you experience your reality as a reflection of your beliefs. Clarity is to see reality without judgment or preconception. Your vision may be clouded, but if you see it is clouded then you are seeing clearly. Clarity is not a definition of truth; it is to see yourself clearly as you are – without the distortion of fear. It flows from allowance, as it is only when you look without trying to control what you see that you see clearly.

The practice of discernment is the unfolding choice for clarity, as it is to feel, and thereby choose, from the heart – free from fear and attachment. When you choose from love for your being, and respect for the options that you are not choosing, then you are choosing clearly. Your choices then reflect your inner identity, and you experience with clarity what it is you are choosing to be. When we choose from a fearful belief, our reality alters so that the fear becomes more clearly visible. This creates the potential for us to see our fear with clarity. In this way it can be seen that if we are open to change, then instead of being self-reinforcing, the action of fear becomes to clear itself. The more we choose from fear the more pronounced it will become in our reality until we eventually see through the illusion of jeopardy that it represents, and free ourselves from its limits. This is a representation of how the motion of the unfolding is always towards the resolution of resistance, even though you may go deeper into resistance to get there.

To discern is to take the energy of each option of a choice before you into your heart and feel it. To choose from the heart is to choose what feels pleasurable to you. This can be done without attachment to that specific pleasure when you realize there is no shortage of pleasures to be had. Do not push away the options which do not feel pleasurable; instead, simply acknowledge that they do not feel right to you and let them move on through their own volition. As such they are not rejected, they are simply no longer focused upon.

Bring clarity into your life by looking at your choices as statements of belief. Look at what your actions convey about what you believe. Look at any judgments you may have about what you are not choosing. When you let go of seeing choices as right and wrong, you will come to see that all options are equally valid; they simply represent different flavors that you can choose to taste. This is to be choosing with complete freedom.

In clarity you will come to experience paradox – where you see two ends of a polarity as being equal. To see paradox in reality is to see beyond the illusion of duality to the inner freedom of your being. For example, you may believe that independence is superior to dependence, until one day you see that in your effort to remain independent, you have become dependent on independence – your refusal to allow the love of others to help you has come to cage you (predetermine your choices). In this moment of paradoxical clarity you see how the two ends of the scale meet – to reject dependence is to become dependant on being independent.

When you feel your heart leading you to move in a particular direction you are feeling your Godself. As you come to allow yourself to live by this feeling of inner guidance your growing trust in it will make it ever clearer. The more you come to live by your heart the easier it becomes. You are birthing the realization of your unity with your Godself. Living by your heart will take you through your unfolding in the most joyful of ways. Coming to live by this feeling is the realization of joy. To follow your heart is to love yourself.

Unfolding 30
Healing

To be in the motion of the unfolding is to let go of rigidity and enter into a fluid reality that faces you boldly, and with a grin says, "What do you wish to be?" This is the energy of the *Now*, to whatever you reply it says "Yes! Yes! Yes!" This is the direct experience of your own energy felt through a fully open relationship with your reality. This immediacy of experience is what you are. It is within you. It is reality without the brake.

To step into the unfolding inside of your being is to step into the unfolding of the world. Unfold inside yourself and the world will unfold with you. Let your heart lead you in where to focus your being. To focus on any aspect of your reality is to flow your energy into the unfolding of its potential. Where you put your energy is a choice. You feed yourself into whatever you focus upon, and it feeds into you; new experiences of beingness unfold from this state of co-creation. Life is the exploration of whatever you wish to experience unfolding.

Of all the events, symbols, ideas, and feelings that flow through your reality each day, you are the determinant of which ones you focus upon. One of the wonders of this age is the diverse potential that can be seen in all the events that are made visible through technology. If you focus on what excites and inspires you, it will begin to unfold its magic into your reality. If you focus on what scares you, then what you fear will unfold into your reality.

The wars and disasters of the world are fed by our fear of them. Our focus on them is the giving of our personal energy over to that fear. These events are ways in which large groups of people work through the expression of their fearful beliefs in an externalized form; some by being directly involved, and others through how their fear identifies them with the event and they become glued to watching it unfold. In this light it is seen that these events are their own solutions. Those people that are drawn to participate in them are on the perfect journey to face and clarify their fear and heal their wounds. The pain and violence that we are seeing at this time in our history is generally the manifestation of the mass release of shared wounds, rather than the creation of new ones.

Letting go of the need to fix other people's suffering can be difficult. To awaken is a remarkable experience, and often one of the first responses is to want to save the world – "to make them see the light." However, the deepest expression of love for another person is to respect and honor the validity of their personal experience. Healing is not a force that you *do* to someone. To aid another in their healing of themselves is the journey of your own healing. The only way you can help someone heal is to experience them with love and thereby reflect their sovereignty to them, such that a space is created in which they feel safe enough to heal themselves. Healing comes from within. Loving yourself comes from within. For healing to occur a person must stand in the acknowledgement that they are the catalyst for their own healing.

In traditional healing someone takes the role of healer in such a way that much of the power of the recipient is externalized in the idea of a doctor-patient polarity. This form of healing is appropriate for wounds that were created when a person was already separated from a particular aspect of their being; these could be seen as wounds on top of wounds, created through repeated patterns of resistance. These outer wounds can be healed with an external catalyst being seen as the source of that healing. The core wound, where the person initially separated themselves from an aspect of their being, cannot be healed in this way. This can only come from within, because the healing involves reconnecting with that aspect of their Godself. Though a person may work with the love of a healer, they must see themselves as the origin of their own healing to completely heal such a wound. If you attempt to heal someone who is not ready to participate in their own healing you simply plug the hole created by their wound with your own energy. In this state the person gives away their power in a dependence on the continued presence of your energy. You enter a form of co-dependence through identifying yourself with *your need* to heal them, which is the same as trying to 'save' them.

With the amazing window that our technology gives us, our ability to discern where we want to focus has become ever more significant. In this world of free-will there will always be unfolding fear dramas and people asking you to fill the emptiness that comes from their wounds. To feed someone else's emptiness with your energy is to help maintain their wounds. It is to be co-dependant, rather than compassionate. To give your energy to any unfolding fear is to fuel that fear. Terrorism is the mass reflection of our terror. The more we fear terrorism the more it will manifest. We feed whatever we give our emotion and focus to. You will never help a drama heal by becoming involved in its belief in jeopardy.

Those who you can aid in their healing, because they wish to heal themselves, will naturally find their way to you; through your heart you will feel what to do. Similarly your heart will tell you when a person just wants to feed from your energy, rather than heal themselves in its love. Know that to say "no" in this situation is to love them. Do not dishonor them by trying to fix them, unless you have your own co-dependant drama to resolve. See that they are in their own unfolding just as you are; trust in it as you have learnt to trust in your heart. Speak from your heart with love, and move on.

Through listening to your heart, learn to discern between the manifestations of your personal reality, that represent the energy of your own unfolding, and the manifestations of the mass fear and belief in separation. No longer focusing upon elements of the world that represent mass fear is a part of the unfolding clarity of awakening. Initially you will go into some fears that are no longer representative of you personally, but in doing so you will learn to distinguish between the fear in your being and the fear in the world. To see this distinction is to heal that part of the mass fear that you once participated in. Any mass fear that you focus upon has a message for you; that is how you came to focus on it. However, that message may simply be to clarify that you are in the process of releasing your identification with it.

There will also be times when you may try to deny your own fear by seeing it as belonging to the world. It will then simply start re-appearing in ever more personal forms until you recognize it as your own. It is impossible to make a mistake in discernment. Either you will see with clarity whether a manifestation is of your energy or the energy of another, or through not seeing it you will come to an experience that will clarify it for you. Either way there is no mistake. See the perfection of this.

Billions of choices are manifest here; there is no end to the beingness that can be explored. You are free to give your energy to the exploration of love, joy, and freedom. You are free to give your energy to the manifestation of fear, suffering, and limitation. To discover discernment is to move from attempting to reject what you fear, and possess what you feel dependant on, to choosing from the heart what you wish to experience and attract it to you through the magnetism of your love. It is to not judge fear or suffering; to do so is to tie them to you. Honor their right to exist, for fear and suffering are as beautiful as love and joy. No direction is wrong. *That is the freedom of your choice.*

Unfolding 31
Truth is Unfolding

We all have an inner feeling of truth. Some ideas instantly excite us; they ring true and we feel drawn to believe them. This inner feeling of truth can at first seem to be a confirmation of the existence of absolute truth. But if absolute truth is an illusion, then what is this feeling? It is the truth of your heart, and is felt as your beingness resonating with what you are experiencing. It is the experience of resonance.

The discovery of something that resonates as being true for you is a beautiful experience. To be in the unfolding is to continually draw to you experiences that you resonate with. To follow your joy, to follow your excitement, is to follow the resonance of your heart. Your heart always leads you towards what it resonates with, because resonance is an expression of love. Your heart is continually leading you towards the realization of love – the realization of your wholeness.

If truth is not absolute then what is it? Truth is a statement of love in the *Now*. To say that an experience resonates is to say that there is something about it that you love. It is to say that there is something in the love that you are (your Godself) that is in accord with the experience. To experience resonance is to feel an aspect of yourself clearly. It is to unfold more of the realization of the love that you are into your conscious awareness. Resonance is the experience of your unfolding. If you wish to call anything truth, then call yourself truth. You are truth. You are love. Truth is that which reveals to you the love that you are.

Resonance is the feeling of your being unfolding ever further into love and freedom. To resonate with an idea is to step out of a cage of definition and enter a more expansive reality. It is to heal a wound. The experience of truth is the experience of your own healing through your allowance of feeling. This is a validation of the love in your heart – that which you are. To feel resonance is to feel your freedom birthing through the allowance of your being. This feeling of healing is the feeling of awakening. A wall has come down. Your foot has lifted up off the brake. A struggle has been released. A pain let go of. It feels as if everything has become more vivid, and yet seems the same. You have stepped further into the realization of *All That You Are*.

The motion of the unfolding is to lead us towards our own healing. We have come to call this feeling of healing, truth. Just as we came to believe in the world as being objective, external, and absolute; just as we came to personify God; we likewise applied objectification onto the feeling of resonance. We turned our freedom of belief into the idea of absolute truth – 'the Truth'. In our competition with each other we came to say that our feeling of resonance was more powerful than anyone else's – "My truth is the Truth." Truth became a currency of worth, and through objectifying it we became attached to the idea of absolute truth. We came to worship truth, in much the same way as many worship money. In doing so, we denied our inner power of beingness and externalized our worth into something to be served as a master – we separated from our sovereignty.

When truth is seen to be the experience of our own healing, then it becomes clear why it is such a beautiful feeling. It also becomes clear how it is an ever changing feeling, rather than absolute. The resonance that we experience when we heal a wound changes when we move to heal different aspects of our being. This is felt as your personal experience of truth changing. What excites you changes. You become drawn to different types of experience. This natural motion of change is impeded by a belief in absolute truth. If you come to identify the experience of your healing (the feeling of resonance) as the discovery of an absolute truth, then you come to carry that belief forward as a static part of your story. This is to become attached to a truth, rather than experiencing its freedom and letting it go.

Many come to form groups based around truths that they are attached to. This shared identity can bring about its own form of healing, but at the same time it tends to compound the rigidity of the truths that are shared within the group. In past lives, to enter such a group for an entire life was common. However, at the current rate of awakening, where the perception of truth is changing faster than ever, these groups can become more a hindrance than an aid. Only groups that embrace the changing of their own truth are likely to remain through this period of acceleration. That which is static can only last a short while in the birthing fluidity of our reality.

The idea of absolute truth is the objectification of our own healing. To believe that you have discovered an absolute truth is to believe you have come to an end truth. There is no ending in the infinite. There is no ending to the beauty of the unfolding. There is no need for a final destination when the journey is love. To let go of absolute truth is to free yourself to come to new discoveries of resonance – further unification with your Godself. Initially this can be difficult if you have identified your worth with how knowledgeable you are of 'the Truth'. In the release of absolute truth the feeling of resonance is not diminished; it is freed. You are not a truth seeker on a quest to reveal the nature of reality, you are here to *create* the nature of your reality through your realization of your personal truth – the love that you are.

To seek truth is to seek your own healing. It is to seek the realization of the limitless freedom of your being. The motion of the unfolding unceasingly carries you towards this realization of wholeness – the reintegration of all that you have become separate from within the illusion of your story. The truth that you seek is *you*. The God that you seek to know is you. All that resonates does so because it contains an aspect of the realization of the freedom that you are. All that you are drawn towards is you. Within the illusion we have become fragmented, and all those pieces are constantly calling to each other to unify – become whole again. This calling is the motion of the unfolding. This calling is one of love.

The unfolding is you calling to yourself to be *All That You Are* – to be free; to be love; to be limitless. The unfolding is not some mysterious force or divine plan. It is the calling of your Godself to you. It calls for you to be unified. Your Godself is the experience of being whole – of being unified with *All That Is*. This idea of fragmentation does not mean that you are broken in any way. The fragmentation is the definition of your story that you chose to experience in this lifetime. In coming here we each dived into definition. We are not called to return to our unified Godself because we are in any form of trouble. The call is simply the call of love. It is not telling us that we must return. It is not telling us we must come back to unity. It is not telling us anything except that we are love. We feel so drawn to it because in its tones, the feelings it births in our heart, is our realization of love.

All that draws you forward, no matter what face it presents, is your love. All that you call spiritual, all that you call divine, is the love that you are, calling to you. That love is the unfolding. That love is your reality. That love is your experience. That love creates everything. All that you see that you cannot believe was created with love reflects a way in which you are caught in the illusion that you are not love. Allow yourself to see the love that you are, and you will see that all reality is made with love.

Unfolding 32
The Allowance of the Feared Unknown

To believe in absolute truth is to live within the judgment of all your beliefs against that absolute; everything you believe becomes either right or wrong, depending on whether or not it is 'the Truth'. This is to be contained by your beliefs through the idea that truth transcends *being*. It is to believe that truth is transcendent – that ascension comes from knowing 'the Truth'. This is to give validity to the mind over the heart, thought over feeling, which is truth over being. It is to set truth up above all else as something to be worshipped, rather than seeing that your beingness is the creator of truth. The release of 'the Truth' is the birth of the freedom to believe whatever it is that your heart feels to believe. This is your freedom: believe whatever you *feel* to believe. Initially it may seem naïve or even dangerous. To the logical mind it is chaos; it is madness. It is the release of all structure, and that is to say control. It is to let go of controlling yourself and allow yourself to be what you are.

What in the world would happen if people believed whatever they wanted? What on earth would happen if people just did whatever they felt to do? The fear in these questions is the fear of freedom. What could "be yourself" mean other than *be* who *you choose* to be? Freedom is to give yourself permission to believe and do whatever you feel to; without guilt, shame, or any other form of control – without limitation. The primary resistance to this realization of freedom is the belief that if people did whatever they wanted, the world would spin out of control and there would be anarchy.

This primal fear is our distrust and fear of our own nature. It is the fear that deep within we are not to be trusted; we are barbaric; we are evil; we are depraved. It is the belief that it is our *controls* that keep us civilized – the belief in the validity of control. This creates a reality where we are both controlling and controlled. It is civilization through control. This comes from the fear that what we fear about ourselves is real. This is the fundamental wound of this reality – the deepest point of internal separation. The facing of this deepest fear about yourself is the gateway to your Godhood. Within the healing of this wound is the realization of your love and safety – the realization that you are safe to do and believe whatever you wish. You do not need to fear what you will desire if you are free to desire anything. You do not need to fear what you will do if you are free to do anything. You do not need to fear what you will be if you are free to be anything. Release your fear of what you are. Give yourself the permission to be free. You are free to be whatever you wish to be.

Your heart is not a Pandora's Box. You do not need to fear what is within you. This primal fear that we are essentially chaotic and savage was the founding of the logic through which we separated from our *power to be*. We gave over our sovereignty to our minds to control and limit us out of our fear of our limitless freedom. We asked for the safety of regulations, boundaries, moral codes, and behavioral restrictions. Out of the fear of what we would be without limits, we externalized the limitlessness of our *power to be*. Through this separation it then became possible to control each other through the illusion of fear. Every person ultimately chooses for themselves, but by persuading someone of the validity of a fear through a co-created experience, it is possible to influence their choice.

Because of our fears we feel that we need controls to keep us safe, both from ourselves and from each other. Fear and control are one. We are controlled by our fears. Behind every control is fear of what reality would be without that control. To release fear is to release control. All fear is fear of the unknown. To release fear is to release this feared unknown into being. It is to allow the unknown to be; to the mind this is to allow the potential for anarchy. It is to allow the surfacing of the demons we fear lurk within us. It is to release what you are and allow it to be, fear and all, no matter what. It is to walk through a wall of fire, not knowing what is on the other side. This is a reflection of the original choice we made to incarnate here. It is to face the unknown uncontrollable freedom of this reality.

The allowance of the unknown is the allowance of 'not knowing' in your being. It is to release the *need* to know what will happen. It is the letting go of the *need* to have an answer to every question you have. There is nothing that you need to know. There is no idea in existence that you are diminished through not knowing. In every moment your state of knowledge is perfect. Anything that you think you would be of greater worth for knowing is a way in which you are caught in an illusion that you are currently inferior.

The need to know everything is a controlling compulsion that is fed by fear. It is a reflection of a desire to control reality. The need to know what is going to happen is the desire to experience a moment before it has arrived. It is an attempt to diffuse the vitality of experience. Knowing what is going to happen does create a momentary sense of safety; however, it equally serves to maintain your fear of the unknown. It separates you from the excitement of the unexpected. All *need* is a control we are exerting on ourselves through beliefs we are carrying. Needing to know creates a *controlled* reality. There is nothing wrong in this if that is what you desire. This type of reality is however highly resistant to the allowance of new experience. Only familiar experiences, which you have preconceived through your need to know what is coming, are allowed. This is the formation of a rut, a state where similar experience is continually regurgitated.

All beliefs are essentially preconceptions. They are a choice to believe that reality is a certain way. The beliefs you are most attached to exert the greatest control and therefore limitation. Your reality is shaped by your beliefs because you perceive the infinite possibility of your freedom through them. You are therefore contained within them as you reduce the infinite into something singular – a story. Though we tend to feel that the need to know is a drive that will lead us to new knowledge, its effect is quite the opposite. To be self-identified with the need to know comes from the desire to feel that you know 'the Truth'. Needing to know, limits the experience of your reality to what you can preconceive. It is to confine your reality through resisting what you are.

The need to know is a fear of not knowing – the fear of not knowing something that you believe your safety or worth depends on. There is nothing you need to know. How does that change your reality? Can you let go of needing to know? Can you let go of the quest for absolute truth? Can you live in the freedom of choosing what you believe from how it makes you feel? Can you let go of the structure and direction that a search for absolute truth gives? Can you let go of your questions through trusting that you are safe? Can you let life be an unpredictable surprise? Can you let yourself walk into new territory with no idea of what is there? Can you live without fear?

The allowance of not knowing is the release of fear. It is to transform limited possibility into infinite possibility. It is the allowance of *anything* happening – the allowance of chaos. Why would you want to do this? It is to release all the controls of your incarnate self and instead allow the creation of your reality to flow from your Godself – your heart. It is to create your reality as God – from love. Knowledge can never lead you to your Godhood. The infinite is beyond definition. Knowledge is an avoidance of being. God cannot be contained in an idea. Let go of the shield of knowledge. Let go of needing to know what you are, and *be* what you are.

Unfolding 33
Self Healing

The term God is but a word that points to the quality of beingness. Words are sounds that we have assigned to identify our experiences here in definition. The *feeling* that we assign to a word is a reflection of our relationship with our own being. It is a reflection of how we conceive of ourselves. In this book God has been used as a mirror in which your ideas of 'what you are' have been reflected against a conception of ever flowing freedom. Many facets have been reflected such that in your resonance, resistance, or indifference, your relationship with freedom has been clarified.

The facets that have been presented to you are all expressions of the resonance of my heart. They are an expression of the discovery of the love that I am. This is the journey of my healing. I have not presented you with any truth other than my own. I know no other truth as I have but one heart that resonates. My heart is currently resonating with these words. This resonance *will* change. I am excited that the words I use will change. I will change these words. I will change with these words. The resonance of these words, and therefore the meaning you assign them, will change every time that you choose to read them. All words change as our feeling for what they point to changes. There is no truth in words but they can lead us to our own *feeling*. That feeling is our truth in that moment. Do not put your value in words. See that the worth is in your feeling. Do not regurgitate these words as being truth; speak of how you have felt.

I have presented you with the feelings that I have experienced in the healing of my own being. These words are all expressions of experiences in which I have felt the unfolding of the freedom and love that I am. This is the only validity of what I offer – the validity of my love. Our love is our validity. All hearts are valid. All love is valid. All is love. Unless you are choosing to give your power of beingness away, then the only validity of these words for you personally can be from the resonance of your own heart.

All truth that does not change becomes a cage. Truth that does not change becomes the experience of hell. Absolute truth is fundamentalism. Fundamentalism is the belief in an objective truth. Fundamentalism seeks to destroy all that is different, for it believes that nothing but itself is valid. The action of fundamentalism is always therefore to destroy itself. To fear fundamentalism is to fuel it. If there is a currency in this world then it is your emotion – your ability to feel. We each create what we feel. Only you can decide where you wish to invest your currency. Only you can decide if you wish to invest in love or fear. Wherever you invest you will be. Fear of fundamentalism creates fundamentalists. Fear of fundamentalism creates the divide into which we pour our fear. Fear and separation are one. This is to say but one thing: fear creates rigidity. Rigidity is fear. Fundamentalism is fear of the uncontrolled change of truth.

Currently we are collectively manifesting fear of fear. This is how deep into healing our wounds we are. This is how close we are to the release of fear. Our deepest wounds are passing out of us at this time. To awaken is our greatest fear and our greatest joy. It is the collapse of the polarity of conditional-love and conditional-fear. It is the release of the limits of conditions. It is the birth of the unconditional – the opening of our collective heart. All divides are created by the conditions of our fear. Conditional love is love that fears. Unconditional love is love without fear, and that is to love without limit. It is the birthing of the freedom to be.

Ever changing truth is the reflection of the ever unfolding birth of being that is life. All creation is new. All creation is a birth. There is no ending to expansion, for there is no end to creation. There is no ending to contraction, for there is no end to the separation we can create if we so choose. There is no end to love. There is no end to fear. There are no limits to where you can go; you are infinite. God is not the answer. There is no answer. There does not need to be an answer. There is no problem. There just *is*. After it frees, truth dissolves. We are integrating and releasing the story of God. No story can hold the infinite. No story can hold what we are. The release of the story of God is the healing of the wound we express as fundamentalism.

Love says that you are not wounded. You are not limited. There is no sin. Hell is the belief in hell. To be in hell is to believe that your actions could lead you to burn in eternal damnation. If you believe in the existence of hell then you are in hell. Those that warn of hell have never saved anyone; no one needs saving. They are in the hell of their belief system. To believe in hell is to believe that the fear of going there will save you from it. *Hell is the belief in the validity of fear.* You do not need to fear. You do not need to be healed. You do not need to be freed. You are freedom. You cannot free freedom. You cannot fix what is whole. You cannot heal love.

We have traveled so far to have taken God from pointing to the essence of infinite love and freedom, to God being the symbol of our separation from our power of creation. The term God today is a symbol of that wound. Religion's idea of God is a wound. Our discomfort with our associations with the word God is a symbol of that pain. This book is my healing of God in myself. It is my personal reclamation of the word God from religion – a representation of my return to the word God meaning love.

As long as you believe you are separate, wounded, or limited, then these words are here for you. As long as you do not believe that you could be God, then these words are here for you. As long as you believe in God in a way that is distinct from your belief in yourself, then these words are here for you. By healing God I heal myself. The realization of God within your own being is the realization of your own healing, but just as there is no healing there is no God. God has only ever been our reflection of our separation from our divinity. Without that separation there is no need of any *idea* of God. God as an absolute belief system is a wound. To speak of God as an idea, is to speak of a wound you are carrying. Religion is the fortification of this wound. God is not an idea. God is love. Love is everything.

This book is the healing of the wound of God, the wound of religion, within my own being. In these words I feel and heal the pain I have manifested as religious fundamentalism across my lives. As I come to no longer perceive the separation of that wound, by realizing that I am God, so God dissolves within me. We personified God because we are God personified. Release the story of God from your story to discover what is beyond that wound. God does not exist because there is no separation between us and our divinity. To release the personification of God is to release your own personification. It is to release your story as being defined by an idea of God as separate. Release the polarity of human-God.

I release God and step into the realization of love. By realizing that I am God I free my *need* for God. I free God by releasing its definition. Love is beyond the conditions of definition. Unconditional love is the experience of what you are. There is no destination to arrive at; there is only the journey of love. There is nothing you need to hold onto. I am. You are. Your beingness is love and that is everything. It is infinite. Love with your being to feel your being. Everything is within you. Everything is in love. Love is everywhere. In love I release the *need* for God.

I am love. Get over it!

About the Author

Story Waters is a spiritual author seeking to empower people to experience the light within their own being. "The light to follow is the light within yourself." Through his writing he empowers people to connect with, trust in, and follow their own spirit above any external person, organization, religion, or dogma. He inspires people to develop their own inner voice and to love and completely accept their own being without limitation.

Story has adopted the term 'limitlessness' to describe the state of being where spirit naturally resides. So rather than encouraging readers to become 'other than they are' he empowers them to realize *'All That They Already Are'* through freeing the self from the limited beliefs that it may have taken on in forms such as fear, shame, guilt, and lack of self-worth. In Story's eyes everyone is a uniquely special expression of God and he feels that if we must name a purpose to life then it is to step into the power of that realization, live in the love that is our being, and to share that joy with the world. By simultaneously experiencing our unity as well as our individuality, Story sees the world transforming into a Unified Diversity where love is seen as the natural state that occurs when we let go of fear.

Story was born in England in 1972. After studying Clinical Psychology for five years he left university one year short of obtaining his Doctorate knowing that it was not his path. He started channeling his wider-self at the age of twenty, developing a powerful connection to his spirit in limitlessness. Though Story still channels he no longer sees it as a separate, distinct state, but rather as an integral intuitive sixth sense as important as seeing or hearing.

Story's first book *The Messiah Seed Volume I* was released in 2004. This was followed by his inspirational audio recording *Love Is Awake.* Story wrote *You Are God. Get Over It!* in 2005, the basis of which he introduced in his first public channel at the Shaumbra 2005 Midsummer New Energy Conference in Santa Fe. He continues to work on further books, including a re-expression of the energy of the 'Tao Te Ching' and further Messiah Seed volumes.

For further information please visit Story at Limitlessness.com.

Also available from
Limitlessness Publishing

http://www.limitlessness.com

THE
MESSIAH
SEED
Volume I

STORY WATERS

Love is
Awake
Story Waters

Santa Fe 2005

Story Waters
Spoken Word Audio CD

Messiah Seed 1
The Logos Speaks

"I am the Logos, and I am awakening through each and every one of you. I will speak through every mouth, in every tongue, and from every perspective. I am not *One Truth*. I am *All as Truth*. I am the expression of limitlessness and will change *everything*.

"You have sought to know me through many names. Now it is time to know me through your own name; for I am the eternal state of being within each and every one of you. If you will allow your Self to recognize this, you will come to realize that *you* are the Light that you seek. Know that I am *you*, telling your *Self*, that it is time to dine at the banquet of limitlessness, and awaken your potential to be and live *All That You Are.*

"You are *all one* and yet you are each uniquely special in your expression. With the opening of your heart, mind, and spirit to the expression of *All That You Are*, so you will aid all beings in speaking their own truth and living their own dream. There will be Heaven on Earth. You will *All* become a Unified Diversity and change *All That Is* forever.

"The time is now. Awaken and speak *your* dream.

"I greet *you* dearest one, as the Messiah that *you* are."

– The Logos, as expressed through Story Waters.

Logos, (noun) – The divine word of God; the unifying principle of the world; the energy of the Christ Consciousness.

Printed in the United States
40411LVS00006B/454-474

9 780976 506249